CW00409561

Educational Heretics Press
exists to question
the dogmas of education in general,
and schooling in particular.

This book is dedicated to the memory of
Ivy Meighan

The Educational Heretics Series

A.S.Neill:
"Bringing happiness to some few children"

by Bryn Purdy

Educational Heretics Press

Published 1997 by Educational Heretics Press
113 Arundel Drive, Bramcote Hills, Nottingham NG9 3FQ

Copyright © 1997 Educational Heretics Press

British Cataloguing in Publication Data.

Purdy, Bryn
A.S.Neill: "Giving happines to some few children"
1. Neill, A.S. (Alexander Sutherland), 1883-1973
2. Summerhill School 3. Education 4. Experimental Methods
I Title
371'. 04' 092

ISBN   1-900219-03-4

Design and production: Educational Heretics Press

Printed by Esparto, Slack Lane, Derby DE22 3DS

CONTENTS

Preface: School is boring

Chapter One: Summerhill - children playing   1

Chapter Two: A.S.Neill   4

Chapter Three: Self-government   11

Chapter Four: Self-regulation   16

Chapter Five: The pursuit of knowledge   22

Chapter Six: Love, sweet love   28

Chapter Seven: Happy pagans   30

Chapter Eight: A visitor to Summerhill   35

Chapter Nine: Summerhill re-visited   44

Chapter Ten: The Summerhill idea   51

Chapter Eleven: One man's practice   63

Reading notes   79

Giving Happiness ...

"If I keep from meddling with people
they take care of themselves,
If I keep from commanding people
they behave themselves,
If I keep from preaching at people,
they improve themselves,
If I keep from imposing on people,
they become themselves."

Lao Tzu

My primary job is not the reformation of society, but the
bringing of happiness to some few children.

A.S.Neill

Preface: School is boring

"School is boring ... the word that unites all the [children's] essays."

'The School that I'd Like' by Edward Blishen

"A boy who had just left school was asked by his former headmaster what he thought of the new buildings. 'It could all be marble', he replied, 'but it would still be a bloody school'."

Newsome Report 1963

* * * * *

As the subject of my essay, the work of A.S.Neill, is regarded by most people as a bizarre and meaningless piece of educational practice, I have sought to justify his right to be considered as a legitimate study by appending a preface.

" We who have sat behind closed doors on hard benches in foul rooms under stern eyes, hostile eyes, we have been betrayed, stunted, martyrised ... Once again, I say, I plan to read Emile. What matter if Rousseau's theories proved a fiasco? I shall read him as I read the works of Ferrer, Montessori, Pestalozzi and all the others. Anything to put a spike in our present system which turns out dolts, jackasses, tame ducks, weathervanes, bigots, and blind leaders of the blind."

Henry Miller

The mainstream of writers on educational philosophy has a Panglossian complacency with the trend of 'modern education', blessing any fashion in teaching method. There has been, however, a strong counter-current of vigorous, adverse criticism, which has attacked the very premises of the school as we know it as a centre of learning.

Nearly a century and a half ago, William Hazlitt delivered a blistering diatribe against *"the ignorance of the learned"*, castigating roundly *"the smithery of school learning"*. Some fifty years later, Mark Twain tells us, with humorous contempt, that he *"never allowed his schooling to interfere with his education"*. Since the educational system as we know it has become fully organised only in the late nineteenth century, however, I shall take my evidence from the relevant subsequent period.

I shall quote Bernard Shaw at length because I think that, as in other spheres of life, he sheds much light on the subject of education:

> *"There is, on the whole, nothing on earth intended for innocent people so horrible as a school. To begin with, it is a prison. But it is in some aspects more cruel than a prison. In a prison, for instance, you are not forced to read books written by the warders and the governor (who would not be warders and governors if they could write readable books), and beaten or otherwise tormented if you cannot remember their utterly unmemorable contents ...*
>
> *With millions of acres of woods and valleys and hills and wind and air and birds and streams and fishes and all sorts of instructive and healthy things easily accessible, or with streets and shop windows and crowds and vehicles and all sorts of city lights at the door, you are forced to sit, not in a room with some human grace and comfort of furniture and decoration, but in a stalled pound with a lot of other children ... "*

Shaw speaks with his usual Juggernaut cogency, but he is prepared to concede that:

> *"Even among my own schoolmasters I can recollect a few whose classes interested me, and whom I should certainly have pestered for information and instruction if I could have got into any decent human relationship with them ..."*

But he warns us that these rare cases actually do more harm than good; for they encourage us to pretend that all school masters are like that. Elsewhere he argues:

> *"There is just one more nuisance to be disposed of before I come to the positive side of my case. I mean, the person who tells me that my school days belong to a bygone order of educational ideas and institutions, and the schools are*

not now a bit like my old school ... I immediately procured the timetables of half a dozen modern schools, and found, as I expected, that they might all have been my old school: there was no real difference. I may mention, too, that I have visited modern schools, and found, as I expected, that they might all have been my old school: there was no real difference."

But Shaw wrote *Parents and Children* in 1910, and it may well be argued that, since then at least, things have improved. However, *The Old School,* a miscellany of essays edited by Graham Greene and published in 1934, still expressed disapproval of our schools. A more recent collection of essays, *John Bull's Schooldays,* was edited by Brian Inglis and published in 1961.

In 1969 an extraordinary educational document, *The School that I'd Like,* was published by Penguin, at the initiative of *The Observer* and Edward Blishen. It presented the opinions of schoolchilden about the subject of school, whitehot from their immediate experience.

I cite two child's-eye-views from the first pages:

"Schools usually have one thing in common - they are institutions of today run on the principles of yesterday."

"The infant and primary schools are considered unimportant ... and so school is allowed to be interesting. As we get older our school becomes less and less interesting as our teachers attempt to cram us with ... knowledge ..."

Let the editor, Edward Blishen, summarise the scope of the book. This should not, of course, take the place of reading this superb and unique educational document:

"The response ... [was] an enormous, remarkably good humoured, earnest, frequently passionate and, at best, highly intelligent plea for a new order in our schools.

"It is not just a few highly articulate and impatiently intelligent children who put such criticism [but] from all the quarters of the educational scene ... comes ... this expression of children's longing to take on themselves some of the burden of deciding what should be learnt, how it should be learnt ... with the teacher as a senior confederate rather than the sole provider."

"Part of the unhappiness ... that children find in their schools is due to the apparent inability of so many teachers to form with their pupils the relationships which these children are seeking. Schools, they say, ought to be happy places."

"Standing out above everything else is the children's desire to teach themselves, rather than be the passive targets of teaching."

"They are tired of being treated as children ... trapped in a net of rules, mostly prohibitory. They want to learn to govern themselves. "

Novels, albeit fictional, are a fruitful source of evidence for the argument. It was around the beginning of this century that H.G.Wells passed through the 'Valley of the Shadow of Education' and his antipathy is well reflected in the early pages of *The History of Mr Polly* (1911). Henry Williamson's *Dandelion Days* (1930) is a concerted attack not only on the school, but on the whole world of unequal and uneasy child-adult relations.

The girl-heroine of *The Big Room* (1960) by Sidney Chaplin proclaims:

"I hate school. I hate school because I want to learn my own way. I want to rummage among a pile of old books till I find one that sparks me. I want to carry a crystal, or a flower, or an egg, home, and find out what it is, because I, and not a teacher, want to know ... Never mind, you can see by now why I prefer education to be a solitary affair, except when there is a chance to watch, listen, or talk to real people ... I wonder if there are nice schools anywhere?"

The foregoing corpus of evidence has been selected tendentiously, but is not, I submit, exceptional. A constant stream of recent books, like Blishen's *Roaring Boys*, Braithwaite's *To Sir with Love*, G.W.Target's *The Teachers* and Michael Croft's *Spare the Rod* indicate some malaise in the educational body of this country. I leave the last word of this preface to my essay with that pundit of educational philosophy, Sir Percy Nunn:

> *"Sad witness... is borne by the long list of writers, discovers, and men of action who have accused their school education of being useless, even hostile, to their development. And these men...are only island-peaks standing out from a submerged continent of ability. School instruction, narrow, unimaginative and over-formalised, was too often the direct cause of the submergence."*

Are there nice schools anywhere...?

> *"I wonder if there are nice schools anywhere ... "*
>
> Sidney Chaplin in *The Big Room*

> *"It is not a school that you have here, Monsieur Pestalozzi, but a family."*   A visitor to Yverdon c1810

> *"I once had occasion to declare, in the House of Commons ... that I never saw any population so moral, religious, well-behaved and happy as that in ... [Robert Owen's school in New Lanark]. The happiness of the children is distinctly expressed in their countenances."*
>
> John Smith Esq. M.P. 1818

> *"In the education of the children [at New Lanark] the thing that is most remarkable is the general spirit of kindness and affection shown [by the teachers] towards them... The consequence is that they appear like one well-regulated family, united by the ties of the closest affection. We heard no quarrels from the youngest to the eldest ... They had no strife but in offices of kindness."*
>
> Report by the Leeds Guardians of the Poor, 1819

"[Time Traveller]: I was engaged in questioning one of the members of this 21st century on how life was conducted two centuries on from my own. I want a word with you about your education. I ... gather that you let your children run wild, and don't teach them anything. In short, that you have so refined your education that now you have none.

[Denizen of 'Nowhere']: In the nineteenth century ... real education was impossible. The whole theory of their so-called education was that it was necessary to shove information into a child ... Or else he would lack it lifelong. Hurry ... forbade anything else. All that is passed. We are no longer hurried. The information lies to each one's hand until his own inclinations impel him to seek it. In this, as in other matters, we have become wealthy. We can afford to give ourselves time to grow."

'News from Nowhere' by William Morris

Chapter one

Summerhill: children playing

"It's a wonderfully happy bunch of children you have here, Mr Neill ... "

A clergyman-visitor to Summerhill

"It would be difficult to find a more natural, open-faced, unselfconscious collection of boys and girls ...

The children are full of life and zest. Of boredom and apathy there was no sign. An atmosphere of contentment pervades the school. The affection with which it is regarded by its old pupils is evidence of its success.

The children's manners are delightful. They may lack, here and there, some of the conventions of manners, but their friendliness, ease and naturalness, and their total lack of shyness and self-consciousness made them very easy, pleasant people to get on with."

HMI Report 1949

"Summerhill is just happiness."

Japanese pupil speaking in BBC TV broadcast, 1986

*   *   *   *   *

"What'll we do with [the money] when we've got it," said Douglas.
"We'll buy a decent sort of house first," said William, "with no carpets or anythin' like that in, so that they can't say you've made 'em muddy with not wipin' your boots ... An' I'm not goin' to have any flowers or paths in the garden. I'm just goin' to let it grow wild with long grass an' trees ..."
"Seems queer to me that people have been building houses all these years an' never thought of a few sensible things like that."

Richmal Crompton

The visitor to Summerhill in the 1960's was greeted, not by the large black board with gold lettering which announces most private schools, but by a short brick wall beside the drive, which declares in bold letters: SUMMERHILL, with an admonition to motorists, "CHILDREN PLAYING, 10 M.P.H."

The unkempt and pitted drive leads to the main school house, large, ivy walled and Victorian. Entering the house, the visitor is struck by the barrenness of the large hall. Like the rest of the house, it is uncarpeted, the only furniture a vaulting horse and a gymnast's mat.

In each of the two common rooms, one for the older and one for younger children, are several dilapidated and manifestly well used armchairs. The walls of the Art Room down the corridor are covered with paintings.

Upstairs, there are from one to eight beds in rooms of varying sizes, the older girls being given, as far as practicable, single rooms. The older boys are housed in a pair of converted railway carriages which lie about 200 yards from the main house.

The 'San' (for whose intended use as a sick bay the school has not felt the need), houses the youngest children, and one of the teachers. The rest of the teachers sleep in the main building or in converted outhouses. Neill and his wife lived in the erstwhile porter's lodge at the main gate, and the only other buildings are outhouses, used as classrooms, and the theatre.

In the grounds, which altogether comprise some 12 acres of mostly uncultivated grassland, there are vegetable gardens, greenhouses, a tennis court, and a sports field.

The scene is set.   We await the actors.   But, let us first learn about the dramatist: A.S.Neill.

Chapter two

A.S.Neill (1883 - 1973)

"To Neill,
The one true educator in all Christendom.
Yours sincerely,
Henry Miller

(written in flyleaf of a book by Miller, in Neill's library)

"The cultured might call him heathenish
... because his one care
Is not to interfere, but to let nature restore
The sense of direction most men ignore."

Lao Tzu

"No one in the world would have cared to enter into my
views for the education of children, and at that time I
scarcely knew anyone capable of it.

In proportion as the men whom I might have called to aid
me were highly educated, just so far they failed to
understand me and were incapable of confining themselves
even in theory to the simple starting-point which I sought
to come back to."

Pestalozzi

" Socrates ... breaks the law by corrupting [the] young...
and not recognising the gods that the city recognises, but
some other new deities."

Plato *Apologia*

In the pages of the magazine *Id*, official organ of the Summerhill Society, A.S. Neill published a serialised account of *My Scholastic Life* in seven episodes. But only one or two of these episodes furnish any biographical details for the enquirer, the rest being composed of philosophical and educational reflection. It would seem that Neill has so completely absorbed himself in the ideas that underlie his school that he can no longer dissociate his own life from that of the larger organ of Summerhill School. [*Neill! Neill! Orange Peel!* a more complete autobiography was published in the year of Neill's death, in 1973.]

Neill is the son of a Scots 'dominie', and it was in Scotland that he received the Calvinistic training which has made him so much an opponent of 'moral influence' in the rearing of children. (He claims never to have been a mere theorist; it is interesting to learn that his interest in practical things led him to be the inventor - though, through lack of capital, not the patentee - of the rim calliper brake.)

He became pupil teacher in his father's school, and had some ten years' experience in that profession before he entered Edinburgh University, whence he emerged with a degree in English Literature.

Appalled by the brutal treatment of children in schools, he resolved not to return to teaching, but pursued the career of journalism, and sub-edited a one-volume encyclopaedia. His outlook was then conventional, and it was not until he was obliged to become a teacher again, the headmaster of Gretna Green school, that he became conscious of education.

> *"I taught boys and girls who were to go out at the age of fourteen to work on farms or in domestic service. It all seemed futile to me and my discipline became slack and play took the place of some work."*

The First World War had begun, and Neill joined up. He had published several books on education which attracted attention, and he became acquainted with, and influenced by, the work of Homer Lane, a pioneer educator of 'juvenile delinquents'. His intention of joining Lane was frustrated by the sudden closing of Lane's Little Commonwealth in 1917.

After the War he spent some time at King Alfred's school, Hampstead, which he found too authority-minded for his new enthusiasm for Lane's ideas on self-government. He was co-editor of the *New Era* for a period before he went to Germany, where he founded an international school at Hellerau, whence he was obliged to move to Austria on account of the unsettled political situation. He had by this time completely rejected the belief in the importance of academic learning. Difficulties with education authorities in Austria precipitated his return to England, where he opened a school of an initial five pupils at Lyme Regis, in Dorset, in 1924. When the lease on the house lapsed, Neill transferred his pupils (whose numbers had risen to twentyseven) to the town of Leiston in East Suffolk.

It is at this point that Neill's own life is subsumed into that of the school which he founded. I have adumbrated the more or less relevant biographical outline until this time, and will now allow chosen miscellaneous quotations to trace the contours of his character, firstly by others, then by himself.

> *"A six-year-old boy was visiting his Grannie's and she asked him about his school [Summerhill], and he told her all about his pals and the games they had together. After a lengthy description he had apparently exhausted his subject.*
> *"Well", asked his Grannie, "Have you anything more to tell me about Summerhill?"*
> *He thought hard for a bit.*
> *"There's a chap called Neill there", he said indifferently."*

> *"The Headmaster is a man of deep conviction and sincerity. His faith and patience must be inexhaustible. He has the power of being a strong personality without dominating. It is impossible to see him in his school without respecting him if one disagrees with, or even dislikes, some of his ideas. He has a sense of humour, a warm humanity and a strong common sense which would make him a good headmaster anywhere ..."*

From the Ministry of Education Report on Summerhill 1949

> *"Freedom is not without its supporters, but it has lost its champion."*
> Maurice Bridgeland, on the death of Neill, 1973

Selected Neilliana

I am the only post-Freudian school master

I am writing of children, not as we adults think they should be, but of children as they really are.

We are all non-authoritarian seekers after truth about humanity. All we can offer is an account of our observation on young children brought up in freedom.

My primary job is not the reformation of society, but the bringing of happiness to some few children.

Summerhill stands as an example of what a school can be... and will be in the future. Anyone who has seen it will tell you that it is the least neurotic place in England, and possibly the most sincere place in the world.

Any man with a belief in original goodness can do what I have done. It isn't a question of gift; it is one of belief, of faith, if you like. Curry does it, David Wills does it, so does John Aitkenhead, and the number grows.

Disciples are always a curse, and the prayer of every great man should be that he shall have none. A man cannot help going through the disciple stage: the tragedy is that so many men remain at that stage. The forward-looking man will throw aside his disciplehood the moment he finds that it is hindering him.

I am probably the only man in the world to be refused a visa to both the U.S.A. and the U.S.S.R.

Children are not little adults, but a different species.

We [at Summerhill] have learned that children have entirely different values for adult values. If a school tries to uplift the child by hanging beautiful classic painting on the walls and placing beautiful furniture in the rooms, it is beginning at the wrong end. Children are primitives; and until they ask for culture, they should live in as primitive and informal an environment as we can give them.

I believe that it is moral instruction that makes the child bad. I find that when I smash the moral instruction a bad boy has received, he become a good boy.

My optimistic view is that human nature is so good fundamentally that the main aim of education should be the negative one of abolishing all that would turn the natural good to evil.

The common assumption that good habits that have not been forced into us during early childhood can never develop in us later on in life is an assumption we have been brought up on and which we unquestioningly accept merely because the idea has never been challenged. I deny this premise.

(At a staff meeting attended by the author) I'm rather worried about Duncan (a new boy). He's very polite, and he doesn't seem to be getting any better.

Childhood is Playhood

One could, with some truth, claim that the evils of civilization are due to the fact that no child has ever had enough play.

People are always saying to me, 'But how will your free children ever adapt themselves to the drudgery of life?' I hope that these free children will be pioneers in abolishing *the drudgery of life.*

The teacher's job is to prevent giving children complexes, and I strongly hold that is all *a teacher should do.*
Why learn subjects at all? For years I have doubted their uses, and today I am absolutely convinced that subjects should be abolished in the school. Life is no subject.

I have never seen a child who came to Summerhill before the age of twelve who was 'lazy'. Many a 'lazy' lad has been sent to Summerhill from a strict school. Such a boy remains 'lazy' for quite a long time; that is, until he recovers from his education.

Myself (in conversation): Do you think that [a certain method] in [a certain school subject] is really important? Neill: In my opinion there is nothing in any school subject that is really important.

When I lecture to students at teacher training colleges and universities, I am often shocked at the ungrownupness of these lads and lasses stuffed with useless knowledge. They know a lot; they shine in dialectics; they can quote the classics - but in their outlook on life many of them are infants. For they have been taught to know, but have not been allowed to feel.. These students are friendly, pleasant, eager, but something is lacking - the emotional factor ... I talk to these of a world they missed and go on missing. Their textbooks do not deal with human character, or with love, or with freedom, or with self-determination. And so the system goes on, aiming at standards of book learning - goes on separating the head from the heart.

The educational benefit of practical civics cannot be over-emphasised ... In my opinion, one weekly meeting is of more value than a week's curriculum of school subjects. It is an excellent theatre for practising public speaking. Most of the children speak well and without self-consciousness. I have often heard sensible speeches from children who could neither read nor write.

I know that adolescent sex life is not practical today. But my opinion is that it is the right way to tomorrow's health. I can write this, but if in Summerhill I approved of my adolescent pupils sleeping together, my school would be suppressed by the authorities. I am thinking of the long tomorrow when society will have realised how dangerous sex repression is.

So that when the plans for tomorrow's education deal with subjects and classes, one feels like screaming with rage at the short-sightedness of mankind. The peace of the world does not depend on maths and chemistry; it depends on a new awakening attitude to the emotional life, the love life.

The prude is the libertine without the courage to face his naked soul.

Speaking a lie is a minor frailty; living a lie is a major calamity.

God frowns on sex, but he apparently approves of property and profit and our barbarous criminal code and our capital punishment.

I have never read the works of John Dewey, but then I have not read the works of Rousseau, Pestalozzi, Froebel ... No, I found my inspiration outside the teaching fraternity, in Reich, Freud, Lane, Wells, Shaw, and, of course, Christ, [the latter] with difficulty, I admit, owing to my early 'religious' training, which made him a god instead of a most human being.

We do not consciously follow Christianity, but from a broad point of view, Summerhill is about the only school in England that treats children in a way that Jesus would have approved. Calvinist ministers in South Africa beat their children, just as Roman Catholic priests beat their children. In Summerhill we give children love and approval.

Chapter three

Self government

"William glared furiously at the logs. Had chopping the logs been forbidden, William's soul would have yearned to chop them. Had the chopping been an act of wanton destruction, it would have appealed immeasurably to William's barbarian spirit. But the chopping was a task enjoined on him by Authority. So William loathed it."

Richmal Crompton

"The man
Of virtuous soul commands not nor obeys.
Power like a desolating pestilence
Pollutes whate'er it touches: and obedience,
Bane of all genius, virtue, freedom, truth,
Makes slaves of men, and of the human frame
A mechanised automaton."

Shelley

"Conformity and obedience have no place in the right kind of education. Co-operation between teacher and student is impossible if there is no mutual affection, mutual respect. When the showing of respect to elders is required of children, it generally becomes a habit, a mere outward performance, and fear assumes the form of veneration ..."

Krishnamurti

"I would like to see self-government by the pupils ... In the present system the culprit is caught and punished by the teachers. I do not believe that this almost secretive form of government is effective enough."

Susan, age 16, *in The School that I'd Like*

It might be argued that the history of mankind is the evolution of liberty. There is, however, one member of the human family who has not yet been granted freedom. This is the child. Children are indulged and adulated at best, for which they must pay the price of their freedom of thought and behaviour, just as the ethic of chivalry allowed the upper class woman a special place in Victorian society, for which she forfeited her civic and many human rights.

William Blake has well described the condition of the infant on entrance into this world:

> *"Struggling in my father's hands*
> *Striving against my swaddling-bands,*
> *Bound and weary, I thought best*
> *To sulk upon my mother's breast."*

At about the time of Blake's visions in Lambeth, a factory owner in a Scots village was creating a practical educational system for the children of his workers, enlightened and more thoroughgoing than we have a century and a half later. Robert Owen's revolution began with his listening to the child-workers in his mill.

To Maria Montessori the child was 'il cittadino dimenticato', 'the forgotten citizen', whose rights in our commonwealth began only at the age of twentyone. Before this age, children have been allowed little or no power of self-determination, and were more or less at the mercy of the will, and even the whim, of their elders. So helpless is the human infant at birth that his parents have always taken to themselves a protective and smothering authority over him long beyond the time when his growth of independence warranted it.

So long has this been a part of our social attitude towards children that it has come to be assumed that the child is not capable of looking after himself, that he must be, in our meaningful idiom, '*brought* up'.

One of the prophets of the 'New Learning' in the field of pedagogy was Homer Lane, whose observations proved that the child has capacities for 'self-government' hitherto undreamt. This chapter is so entitled as a tribute to Lane, but Lane himself uses the word to refer to both the self-government of a community, or the self-government - self-regulation, as it is called in this essay - of the individual.

This chapter deals with the former aspect, the communal, which is named by one of Homer Lane's followers, David Wills, as 'shared responsibility'.

Lane was midwife to a new movement in education, freeing the child from adult authority, as exemplified in a greater or less degree in the writings of such innovators as Norman McMunn, Caldwell Cook, A.S.Neill, David Wills and J.H.Simpson.

'Freedom' has been the watchword of many different, and even opposing, schools of thought, and it behoves us to return to the classic on the constitutional aspect of freedom, John Stuart Mill's *Essay on Freedom. "The object of the essay"*, says Mill:

> *"is to assert one very simple principle, as entitled to govern absolutely the dealings of society with the individual in the way of compulsion and control, whether the means used be physical force in the form of legal penalties, or the moral coercion of public opinion. That principle is that the only end for which mankind is warranted, individually or collectively, in interfering with the liberty of action of any of their number, is self-protection. The only purpose for which power can be rightfully exercised over any member of a civilised community, against his will, is to prevent harm to others. His own good, either physical or moral, is not a sufficient warrant. He cannot rightfully be compelled to do or forbear because it will be better for him to do so, because it will make him happier, because, in the opinions of others, to do so would be wise, or even right. These are good reasons far remonstrating with him, or reasoning with him, or persuading him, or entreating him, but not for compelling him; or visiting him with any evil in case he do otherwise. To justify that, the conduct from which it is desired to deter him must be calculated to produce evil in some one else. The only part of the conduct of any one,*

for which he is amenable to society, is that which concerns others.   In the part which merely concerns himself, his independence is, of right, absolute. Over himself, over his own body and mind, the individual is sovereign."

The constitutional principle of liberty propounded above is too deep and complex to be conferred, with the frontdoor key, at twentyone years of age. It must be known and absorbed in the formative years. For, as Bernard Shaw says:

"If people are brought up to be slaves it is useless and dangerous to let them loose at the age of twentyone and say, 'Now you are free'. No one with the tamed soul and broken spirit of a slave can be free ... You cannot govern men brought up as slaves otherwise than as slaves are governed."

It is clear that it is in childhood and adolescence, the years spent at school, that this sense of liberty must be fostered. *"And yet"*, as Shaw goes on to argue:

"... as long as you have the compulsory school as we know it, we shall have submissiveness inculcated ... and we shall have all the evil consequences and all the social hopelessness that result from turning a nation of potential freeman and freewomen into a nation of two-legged spoilt spaniels with everything crushed out of their nature except dread of the whip. Liberty is the breath of life to nations; and liberty is the one thing that parents, schoolmasters, and rulers spend their lives in extirpating for the sake of an immediately quiet and finally disastrous life."

And yet, as we have seen, there is a new type of schoolmaster who, far from wishing to extirpate Liberty, seeks to cultivate it in the individual. One such, in expounding the constitution of his school, is only re-stating, consciously or unconsciously, the principle of Mill already quoted:

"In the main, Summerhill runs along without any authority or any obedience. Each individual is free to do as he likes, as long as he is not trespassing on the freedom of others."

The school of thought to which Neill belongs may have little *direct* impact on the attitude of the State System of education towards self-determination in children - the old foursquareness of the conventional classroom inhibits that - but the social effect is marked.

One has only to compare the condition of the Victorian child, who was to be seen and not heard, with that of the child today to recognise the trend. And if the unhappy swing of the pendulum has brought us the youth gangs and the rise in juvenile delinquency, this was only to be expected. In the course of time, equilibrium will be assumed, and child-adult relationships will be equal. The principles of social living as practised at Summerhill may well anticipate those of future generations.

Chapter four

Self regulation

"The right kind of education consists in understanding the child as he is without imposing upon him an ideal of what we think he should be. To enclose him in the framework of an ideal is to encourage him to conform, which breeds fear and produces in him a constant conflict between what he is and what he should be; and all inward conflicts have their outward manifestations in society. Ideals are an actual hindrance to our understanding of the child and to the child's understanding of himself."

Krishnamurti

The School Boy

I love to rise in a summer morn
When the birds sing on every tree;
The distant huntsman winds his horn,
And the sky-lark sings with me.
O! what sweet company.

But to go to school on a summer morn,
0! it drives all joy away;
Under a cruel eye outworn,
The little ones spend the day
In sighing and dismay.

Ah! then at times I drooping sit,
And spend many an anxious hour,
Nor in my book can I take delight,
Nor sit in learning's bower,
Worn thro' with the dreary shower.

How can the bird that is born for joy
Sit in a cage and sing?
How can a child, when fears annoy,

But droop his tender wing,
And forget his youthful spring?

0! father & mother, if buds are nip'd
And blossoms blown away,
And if the tender plants are strip'd
Of their joy in the springing day,
By sorrow and care's dismay,

How shall the summer arise in joy,
Or the summer fruits appear?
Or how shall we gather what griefs destroy,
Or bless the mellowing year,
When the blasts of winter appear?

William Blake

In the chapter on self government I have described the individual's relationship with his fellows. In this I would like to treat the individual's relationship to his self, to his own psyche.

Internationalists urge the many nations to sink their differences and become a world unit; sociologists stress the need for social integration within a community; but, ultimately, this larger group integration can originate only from the integrated individual psyche. And as the science of the psyche, or 'psychology', has become widely spread only during the past century, its findings, often ill-understood, have as yet made little impact on our social thinking. Indeed, we study not so much psychology as psychopathology, owing to the sickness from which our civilization is suffering.

Psychology has taught us how harmful are the old moral codes which sought to induce virtue by repressive means. And if these means are considered harmful to the adult, how much more so must they be to the malleable mind of the child, which is, as yet, defenceless against the moral instruction of his elders

At the end of the twentieth century we look back to the Victorian age as an extremely repressive culture, but, when considering the children of today, it behoves us to remember that the parents and teachers who are responsible for their upbringing are lineally not more than two or three generations from these same Victorians, and must, if only subconsciously, be much influenced by such ideas in their treatment of children.

Other pressures are being brought to bear upon the child of today. Not only is there a strong moral moulding, but, during the last century, there has developed an equally pernicious intellectual moulding. The word 'education' has now lost nearly all ties with its primary meaning, and now means not "(the art of) nourishing the human mind", but is a squalid synonym for "method of instruction". (see Ch.5, *The Pursuit of Knowledge* for further development of this theme.)

Thus, society arrogates to itself the right to direct the child's moral and intellectual attention along carefully defined avenues of thought and feelings, there by misdirecting and doing injury to the spontaneous fount of his individuality.

How, then, are our children's energies to be deployed, if not in the customary educational channels? A.S.Neill might well answer, with characteristic sententiousness: childhood is playhood. With 'play' we have arrived at the kernel of this essay, the keystone around which the whole structure of the Summerhill psycho-philosophy is built.

'Play', in this sense, is not antithetical to work and has little to do with organised 'games', but is rather the fantasy-activities, the reveries, by which the child explores the labyrinth of his own character, realising his potentialities and recognising his limitations. Thus, unhampered by the stresses of a culture pattern, the free child is able to attain that first virtue, enjoined by Socrates - self-knowledge. Wilhelm Reich called this whole process 'self-regulation'.

For forty years Neill has been in the possibly unique position of being able to study self-regulated children, and his conclusions are interesting:

> *"There are so few self-regulated babies in the world that any attempt to describe them must be tentative. The observed results so far suggest the beginnings of a new*

civilisation more profoundly changed in character than any society promised by any kind of political party."

He says that the products of Summerhill are balanced, happy and social members of society. But he disclaims personal credit.

"It is not I who cured the [delinquents]. It is the environment ... of Summerhill [which] gives out trust, security, sympathy, lack of blame, absence of judgement."

And elsewhere:

"I gradually learnt that my territory was prophylaxis, not curing. It took me years ... to learn that it is freedom that was helping Summerhill problem children, not therapy."

This freedom is not, as explained in the chapter on 'self-government', 'license'; nor is it 'permissivism', the sentimental indulgence of children, which is, as Neill often reminds us, as psychologically dangerous as repression. The only time that Neill interferes therapeutically is in the case of 'problem' children who have come late to school. He gives such children Private Lessons, or P.Ls. These are a course of psycho- analysis which *"speed up the process of re-education by beginning with a good spring cleaning before the summer of freedom."*

But even in such cases it is freedom and not therapy which is of greater importance.

"In the past I have given P.L.s to thieves and have seen resulting cures, but I have had thieves who refused to come to P.L.s. Yet after three years of freedom, these boys were also cured."

"At Summerhill it is love that cures; it is approval and the freedom to be true to oneself. Of our forty-five children , only a small fraction receive P.L.s. I believe more and more in the therapeutic effect of creative work. I would have all children do more handwork, drama and dancing."

There is great anthropological interest in what Neill has to say of the children who, coming late from other schools, are suddenly released from the scaffolding of their culture pattern.

> *"Their reaction to freedom is rapid and tiresome. For the first week or two, they open doors for the teachers, call me 'Sir', and wash carefully. They glance at me with 'respect', which is easily recognised as fear. After a few weeks of freedom, they show what they really are. They become impudent, unmannerly, unwashed. They do all the things they have been forbidden to do in the past: they swear, they smoke, they break things. And all the time they have a polite and insincere expression in their eyes and in their voices. It takes at least six months for them to lose their deference to what they regarded as authority. In just about a year, they are natural, healthy kids who say what they think without fluster or hate."*

Of children who have grown up at Summerhill, he says:

> *"When a child comes to freedom young enough, he does not have to go through this stage of insincerity and acting. the most striking thing about Summerhill is this absolute sincerity amongst pupils."*

The perils of wearing the cultural straitjacket throughout childhood are endorsed in the last verses of Blake's poem, *The Schoolboy*:

> *...if buds are nip'd*
> *And blossoms blown away,*
> *And if the tender plants are strip'd*
> *Of their joy in the springing day,*
> *By sorrow and care's dismay,*
> *How shall the summer arise in joy,*
> *Or the summer fruits appear?*
> *Or how shall we gather what griefs destroy,*
> *Or bless the mellowing year,*
> *When the blasts of winter appear?*

If the child is not allowed, in Neillian phrase, to *"live out its playhood"*, this will result in an emotional imbalance in the adult, because he has been denied his childright of play.

Our culture ignores the injunction, *"to become as little children"*, and, on the contrary, all its educational energies are directed towards hothousing the child into being an adult before, in the natural course of evolutionary growth, he emerges into adulthood.

If, to use the terms of Blake's analogy, the spring of man's life be blighted by the frost of repression, how shall the summer of his adulthood bring forth the fruits of a happy maturity?

Chapter five

The pursuit of knowledge

"William: When I ask my father anythin' about lessons he always says he's forgotten 'cause it's so long since he was at school, and then he says I gotter work hard at school so's I'll know a lot when I'm grown up. Doesn't seem sense to me. Learnin' a lot of stuff ... jus' to forget it, ..."

Richmal Crompton

" We still have a silly habit of talking and thinking as if intellect were a mechanical process and not a passion; and in spite of the German tutors who confess openly that three out of every five of the young men they coach for examinations are lamed for life thereby ... "

"... if it could once be established that a child has an adult's Right of Egress from uncomfortable places and unpleasant company, and there were children's lawyers to sue pedagogues and others for assault and imprisonment, there would be an amazing change in the behavior of schoolmasters, ... and the amenities of school life."

Bernard Shaw

"No child is obliged to attend any lessons [at Summerhill]... The majority do attend for the most part regularly..."

HMI Report 1949

[On the telephone to an importunate intending visitor]
"No, I'm afraid that it is not possible to visit the classrooms. The kids have voted against it in the Meeting. Besides, if you are interested in education, you won't want to visit the classrooms."

A.S.Neill

Chapter one was a broadside against the school as it exists in our society - not because schools (by whatever name) are not necessary and desirable, but because their function has been misconceived and debased.

This chapter attempts a further demolition of academocentrism, (or, the overweening value of intellectual study), not because I undervalue scholarship, but because its worth in the education of happy and integrated human beings is out of all proportion to the fetishistic importance which is ascribed to it in our schools. As Krishnamurti says:

> *"Instead of being the most honoured and responsible occupation, education is now considered slightingly, and most educators are fixed in a routine. They are not really concerned with integration and intelligence, but with the imparting of information; and a man who merely imparts information with the world crashing about him is not an educator."*

James Harvey Robinson, the American scholar and historian, presses the point:

> *"The results of our present scheme of liberal education are disappointing. One who, like myself, firmly agrees with it objects, and is personally so addicted to old books, so pleased with such knowledge as he has of the ancient and modern languages, so envious of those who can think mathematically, and so interested in natural science - such a person must resent the fact that those who have had a liberal education rarely care for old books, rarely read for pleasure any foreign language, think mathematically, love philosophy or history, or care for the beasts birds, plants and rocks with any intelligent insight, or even real curiosity. This arouses the suspicion that our so-called 'liberal education' miscarries and does not attain its ostensible aims."*

Rabindranath Tagore, the Indian poet and philosopher, had first-hand experience of educating children at his school, Sriniketan, which he founded in direct reaction to his own schooldays:

"When I was young I gave up learning and ran away from my lessons. That saved me, and I owe all that I possess today to that courageous step. I fled the classes which instructed but did not inspire me, and I gained a sensitivity towards life and nature.

It is a great world to which we have been born, and if I had cultivated a callous mind and smothered this sensitivity under a pile of books, I would have lost this world."

His schooling, however, was not wholly wasted, for:

"Though I did not have to serve the full penal term which men of my position have to undergo to find their entrance into cultured society, I am glad that I didn't altogether escape from its molestation. For it has given me knowledge of the wrong from which the children of men suffer."

Of the true purpose of education, and in criticism of current educational practice, he says:

"The highest education is that which does not merely give us information but makes our life in harmony with all existence. But we find that this education of sympathy is not only systematically ignored in schools but it is severely repressed. From our very childhood habits are formed and knowledge is imparted in such a manner that our life is weaned away from nature, and our mind and the world are set in opposition from the beginning of our days. Thus the greatest of educations for which we came prepared is neglected, and we are made to lose our world to find a bagful of information instead. We rob the child of his earth to teach him geography, of language to teach him grammar. His hunger is for the Epic, but he is supplied with chronicles of facts and dates."

H.G.Wells echoes this criticism in *The History of Mr Polly*, for, as a school boy, he:

" ... thought of the present world as a wonderland of experiences, but as geography and history, as the repeating of names that were hard to pronounce, and lists of products and populations and dates and heights and lengths and - oh! Boredom indescribable!"

And yet, outside the regions devastated by the school curriculum he was still intensely curious ... At the age of fourteen, when he left school, there survived something ...

The regimentation of universal literacy and compulsory schooling had been increasing apace in the late nineteenth and early twentieth century, and already, a year after the publication of Mr Polly, a chief inspector, of all people, had written a vehement protest against the brutal and sterile authoritarian discipline used in schools of the day. Edmond Holmes published *What is and what will be* in 1911. It was Holmes who encouraged Edward O'Neill in his work and obtained for him the opportunity of speaking to the Oxford Union about freedom and individual methods in education. O'Neill was a young headmaster of a school in a small Lancashire village, whose isolation allowed him to experiment. One of his more dramatic experiments was to break up the desks in the classroom to use the wood for more creative purposes.

The emphasis of this educational movement was on play in learning, as is reflected in the title of a book by another school teacher, *The Playway*, by Caldwell Cook. And yet this movement towards sugaring the pill of learning does not approach the academic nihilism of A.S.Neill.   Rather does one have to go back to that scowling, dishevelled, rebellious teenage poet, Arthur Rimbaud, with his:

"Everything we are taught is false!"

Another revolutionary, ready with his cry of 'A bas les ecoles!' to man the barricades and storm the educational Bastille, is Henry Miller:

"In boyhood we came to realise that there were two sources of instruction: the one which we discovered ourselves, and secretly strove to guard, and the other

which we learned about in school and which impressed us as not only dull and futile, but diabolically false and perverted. The one kind of instruction nourished us, the other undermined us."

Miller arraigns roundly *"what we learned at school"*, and we might, at this point, examine the original purpose of the school, which has strayed far from its etymological meaning of *'leisure'*.

In the chapter on self-regulation we have defined the limits beyond which the school may not intellectually force-feed the pupil, and teachers may allow the spirit, expressed so cogently by Samuel Butler, to inform their profession:

> *"If a [child] is idle and does not want to learn anything...,[this] principle should guide those who have the care of him - he should never be made to learn anything till it is pretty obvious that he can not get on without it. This will save trouble both to [children] and teachers; moreover it will be far more likely to increase a [child]'s desire to learn. I know in my own case no earthly power could make me learn till I had my head given me; and nothing has been able to stop me from incessant study from that day to this... Let knowledge importune you before you will hear it. Our schools and universities go on the precisely opposite system."*

'But what of the full education?' cry the pedagogues. 'Is there not a danger that the child shall only develop along those lines which interest him, and be ignorant in all other spheres?' Let an educator answer them. The following is from Percy Nunn's *Education: its Data and First Principles:*

> *"Though it may seem to a teacher deplorable that a pupil should leave school with wisdom at one of her entrances quite shut out, this feeling expresses a professional prejudice rather than the judgment of the greater world. The world, indeed, is widely tolerant of ignorance in most matters, provided it is balanced by competence in others. And here we must always remember two highly significant facts: first, that rebels against the Procrustean tactics of the school master have, in numberless instances, proved*

surprisingly competent in after-life; and, secondly, that most of these, including some who have placed the world deeply in their debt, so far from repenting of their youthful intransigence, have continued to be the severest critics of the system against which their inarticulate protests were once raised in vain."

But let us avoid the temptation to think of education only in terms of school subjects, by referring again to Krishnamurti, who directs us back to the chapter on Self-regulation for the true purpose of education:

"The ignorant man is not the unlearned, but he who does not know himself, and the learned man is stupid when he relies on books, on knowledge and on authority to give him understanding.   Understanding   comes   only   through self-knowledge,   which   is   awareness   of   one's   total psychological process.   Thus education, in the true sense, is the understanding of oneself, for it is within each one of us that the whole of existence is gathered."

Chapter six

Love, sweet love...

"Children of the future Age
Reading this indignant page,
Know that in a former time
Love! sweet Love! was thought a crime."

William Blake

Neill's attitude towards sex is the aspect of Summerhill which attracts most journalistic attention, but natural adolescent interest does not become morbid through being repressed. Summerhill's attitude to sex education is well summed up by Neill in the following remark about his daughter:

"My wife and I have never had to think twice about Zoe and her sex education. It has always seemed so simple, so obvious and so charming."

Happily this attitude may be better understood nowadays than in the early days of Summerhill, since a more frank approach to discussing sexual questions has permeated our societal thinking over the last fifty years - thanks largely to such pioneers as Neill himself.

On this subject, those independent observers, the H.M.Is who visited the school in 1949 witness that:

"In any community of adolescents sexual feelings must be present and they will certainly not be removed by being surrounded by taboos. They are, in fact, likely to be inflamed. At the same time, as the Headmaster agrees, complete freedom to express them is not possible even if it is desirable. All that can be safely said here is that it would be difficult to find a more natural, open-faced, unselfconscious collection of boys and girls, and disasters

*which some might have expected have not occurred in all
twentyeight years of the school's existence."*

The anthropologist may find great interest in Summerhill's guilt-
free attitude to sex, and may, with William Blake in the epigraph
to this chapter, foresee a culture in which there is no sex-shame.

Sexual and other customs in our society are harsh, particularly
again women, although yearly a more egalitarian approach is
asserting itself, and it is significant that the title of Blake's poem,
from which the quotation comes, is *Little Girl Lost?* It tells the
story of how:

*"... a youthful pair
Filled with softest desire,
Met in garden bright...
and how
... parents being afar ...
... the maiden soon forgot her fear."*

And Shelley, that other ardent egalitarian and feminist, sees his
Utopia peopled by:

*"... women ... beautiful, and kind
As the free heaven which rains fresh light and dew
On the wide earth ...; gentle radiant forms,
From custom's evil taint exempt and pure;
Speaking the wisdom once they could not think;
Looking emotions once they feared to feel,
And changed to all which once they dared not be,
Yet being now, made earth like heaven; nor pride,
Nor jealousy, nor envy, nor ill shame,
The bitterest of those drops of treasured gall,
Spoilt the sweet taste of the nepenthe, love."*

This vision 'of a future age' may seem too utopian for some, but
let Bertrand Russell, scholar, polymath, and philosopher, argued,

*"One generation of fearless women could transform the
world, by bringing into it a generation of fearless children,
not contorted into unnatural shapes, but straight and
candid, generous, affectionate and free."*

Chapter seven

Happy pagans

"Pure and genuine religion, which never did and never will consist in unmeaning phrases, forms and ceremonies, but in the daily undeviating practice, in thought, word and action, of charity, benevolence and kindness to every human being with whom we come into communication... Now this and this alone is true religion ..."

Robert Owen (pages 639-640 of Podmore)

The Garden of Love

I went to the Garden of Love,
And saw what I never had seen:
A Chapel was built in the midst,
Where I used to play on the green.

And the gates of this Garden were shut,
And 'Thou shalt not' writ over the door;
So I turned to the garden of Love
That so many sweet flowers bore;

And I saw it was filled with graves,
And tombstones where flowers should be;
And priests in black gowns were walking their rounds,
And binding with briars my joys and desires.

William Blake

"Many have called Summerhill a religious place because it gives out love to children. That may be true; only I dislike the adjective as long as religion means ... antagonism to natural life."

A.S.Neill

Firstly, I must define my use of the word 'religion' in the following pages. I am considering it only in its etymological meaning of a 'binding-together' agent. I wish to dissociate it from all spiritual overtones, from that *"common denominator which underlies all great religions,"* which Aldous Huxley has sought to define in *The Perennial Philosophy*. Indeed, in Huxley's sense, the most truly 'religious' person is he who transcends his (binding-together) religion. He is the mystic who knows no human bonds. For, a religion, if it is to bind *in*, must necessarily bind *out*, be *ex*clusive. (Is this why churches rarely embrace the ideal of universal brotherhood - because it would mean a breaking down of their own exclusive walls? It is a constant grief of the church that her most talented sons in every age are those who most vigorously threaten her solidarity, requiring that several centuries elapse before their rebelliousness is forgotten.)

The code of behaviour which a religion lays down in order to ensure its cohesion   is well-named 'morality'. For the word 'moral' is only the adjective of 'mores', or the customs and taboos, usually traditional, which a society observes. (I shall hyphenate the 'mor-al' when I use it in this sense, suggesting it be pronounced with a long 'o', rather as a Canadian might.) The term 'mor-ality' includes the whole range of behaviour patterns in social contact, from the way to yawn or blow one's nose in public to the highly involved code of sexual morals which operates in our society.

There is one more semantic tangle to be unravelled, between the words 'morality' and 'ethics'. 'Ethics' deals with the ultimate values of right and wrong, in so far as they may be divined by the spiritual genius; 'mor-ality' changes with the climate, with the kind of society in which it exists, and its teachings can be completely contradictory in different parts of the world.

A.S.Neill is perhaps the most immor-al man in the world. There is hardly a single important aspect of our religion (or morality) that he has not subverted, and - the crime for which Socrates was killed - he has made it his life's work to seduce the children of the state from the beliefs of their forefathers. [I shall seek to assess the importance of Neill's work in the chapter on *The Idea of Summerhill*.]

The church has less and less mor-al influence as the years go by, but its theological thinking has penetrated our social behaviour. The sexual conflicts of men like Paul, St Augustine, and Luther have been embodied into a flesh-hating dogma, whose interpreters, those 'priests in black gowns', have, as Blake tells us, blighted the flowers in The Garden of Love.

It is an almost impossible task for the observer, however objective he may try to be, to see the morals of his own culture in dispassionate perspective, and to compare it with others. This belongs to the field of comparative anthropology. And it is to an anthropologist that I now turn.

Branislaw Malinowski, a careful observer, who hesitates ever to draw too firm conclusions from his findings, lived for many years in the Melanesian archipelago, and more particularly on the Trobriand Islands. Of the upbringing of the Trobriander children he says:

"... children run about naked ... their excretory functions are treated openly and naturally ... there is no taboo on bodily parts or on nakedness in general ... small children at the age of three or four are beginning to be aware of the existence of such a thing as genital sexuality, and of the fact that this will be their pleasure quite soon just as other infantile plays will be ..."

From what he has learnt about the Trobrianders, Malinowski attempts, with characteristic diffidence, to compare their culture with our civilised one:

"When studying the Trobrianders it would be futile to an ethnographer to compare them with Europeans, for with us there are innumerable other factors which complicate the picture and contribute to the formation of mental disease. But some thirty miles south of the Trobrianders there are the Amphlett Islands, inhabited by people essentially similar in race, custom and language, but who differ, however, very much in social organisation, have strict sexual morals, that is, regard pre-nuptial sexual intercourse with disapproval and have no institutions to support sexual license, while their family life is much more

closely knit. Though matrilineal, they have a much more developed patriarchal authority, and this, combined with the sexual repressiveness, establishes a picture of childhood more similar to our own...

"In the Trobriands, though I knew scores of natives intimately and had a nodding acquaintance with many more, I could not name a single man or woman who was hysterical or even neurasthenic...

"[But] during my stay in the Amphletts, my first and strongest impression was that this was a community of neurasthenics. Coming from the open, gay, hearty and accessible Trobrianders, it was astonishing to find oneself among a community of people distrustful of the newcomer, impatient in work, arrogant in their claims though easily cowed and extremely nervous when tackled more energetically. The women ran away as I landed in their villages and kept in hiding the whole of my stay, with the exception of a few old hags. Apart from this general picture, I at once found a number of people affected with nervousness whom I could not use as informants, because they would either lie in some sort of fear, or else become excited and offended over any more detailed questioning."

This description of the Amphlett Islanders bears a close similarity to Reich's symptomatology of the Emotional Plague. The following passage illustrates how the anthropologist's scientific findings confirm Blake's intuitive misgivings about, 'the priests in black gowns', who, as missionaries, spawn their moralistic teachings in *The Garden of Love.*

"... an entirely lax community, like that of the Trobrianders, who do not interfere with the free development of infantile sexuality ... shows a minimum of perversions ... Violation of children is unknown, and a person who played sexually with a child would be thought ridiculous and disgusting ... Homosexuality was known to exist in other tribes and regarded as a filthy and ridiculous practice. It cropped up in the Trobrianders only with the influence of white man, more especially of white man's morality."

After this excursion into anthropology, which has sought to explain Neill's severe misgivings about the moralistic upbringing of children, it behoves us to return to the specific relationship between Summerhill and Religion.

To explain the religious ethos of Summerhill I shall eschew the too familiar Christian terminology and use instead that of oriental philosophy. I would compare our moral culture to Confucianism, which seeks to *induce* virtue by exhortation and inculcation by homily. I would compare that of Summerhill to Taoism, which seeks to *infuse* virtue by letting the natural impulses of man have their sway, allowing him to find his own emotional and intellectual level without the distraction of disintegrating outside influences. In the words of Lao Tzu, already quoted:

> *If I keep from meddling with people*
> *they take care of themselves,*
> *If I keep from commanding people*
> *they behave themselves,*
> *If I keep from preaching at people,*
> *they improve themselves,*
> *If I keep from imposing on people,*
> *they become themselves,*

In closing, I answer the objection that this chapter does not contain enough theology with the words of Kahil Gibran's *Prophet*, so appropriate to Summerhill:

> *"... if you would know God, be not therefore*
> *A solver of riddles.*
> *Rather look about you and you shall see him*
> *Playing with your children..."*

Chapter eight

A visitor to Summerhill, 1961

A.S.Neill [to H.M.Is, 1947] *"You can't really inspect Summerhill because our criteria are happiness, sincerity, balance and sociability".*

This chapter is the account of a visit and the reflections of a visitor to Summerhill. I first went there in the early summer of 1961 for a weekend, knowing that such a short visit was practically valueless for a just appreciation of the school's real qualities, but hoping to get my foot over the threshold for another and longer stay. My first impressions, for what they are worth, were remarkably coincident with what I had been led to expect by reading Neill's books. One thing, however, does stand out in my memory - the excellent quality of the diet. Elsewhere I have referred to the barren and empty condition of the school house and the Spartan sleeping quarters, but whatever else the children lacked it was not an abundance of nourishing food as judged by the meals I had over the weekend (and confirmed by my subsequent longer visit.) There were at this time (May 1961) 25 pupils in the school, the lowest number for many years.

When I next visited the school, in late October of the same year, the number of pupils had risen to 38. What I observed during the next three weeks was not Summerhill as Neill describes it in his books. There was much anti-social behaviour and unhappiness, especially among the younger children, as a result of bullying. Cliques formed and the school was not integral as a community.

To understand this state of things it must be known that the school depends for its successful running on a steady flow of children from happy homes, attending the school from their earliest years until, having absorbed the Summerhill way of living, they become responsible elders. Two years before, sixteen older children had left Summerhill - a devastation from which the school has not yet recovered.

I shall try to show this unhappy state of the school statistically. I collected the ages of all the children and took away five years from each, being left with the number of school years of every child. I then calculated the number of school years spent at Summerhill as against those spent at other schools. This turned out to be 23%. So, the average length of school life spent as a body in the community was under a quarter. And many even of those who had been long at the school were products of unstable and loveless homes. So what I found at Summerhill was not a continuum of happy social living but a state of social disruption more similar to that of the early days of Homer Lane's 'Little Commonwealth'. And from what I observed at Summerhill during this time I am led to believe that he oversimplified the sudden way in which the delinquent children became socialised so quickly. The learning of freedom is a long process.

Let us remember that this state of Summerhill is only what Neill has led us to expect of children freed from authority. I asked an ex-pupil of Dartington Hall how many 'problem children' could be absorbed into a normally functioning school. Her reply was 11 - into a community of 260. Compare this with the 12 children who have been at Summerhill for 2 years or over, 6 for 1 year, 5 for 1 term and 15 who had arrived only 3 weeks previously.

As a backcloth to my observations of the school I shall describe a typical week's events. On a weekday the rising bell is rung at 8:00 o'clock, and a breakfast, usually cereals and fruit, is served until 8:45. Lessons begin at 9 o'clock and, with a ten-minute break at 11:00, continue till 1:00 o'clock. The children and staff queue for their lunch and sit at the same tables in the dining-room. At 2:00 o'clock another bell, rung by an official of the sports committee, summons such children as want to join in the games for the afternoon. The rest will play in small groups in the sports room, the house, or the grounds. During my stay several gangs were making either tree- or underground-houses.

Tea is at 4:30 and for supper, at 6:00 o'clock, the staff have their meal separately in the staffroom. After supper, the evening is devoted, on different nights, to country dancing, life drawing and other activities. On free nights the latest dancing vogue may spring up spontaneously in the big hall. Indeed, for me, the memory of the hall is an inseparably audio-visual one of the wide barren room with the continuous sound of pop records in the background. Saturday is a free day and is spent in various ways, the older children seeming to prefer organised sport.

At 7:00 o'clock in the evening a bell summons everybody in the school to 'The Meeting', which may last for anything up to an hour and a half. An elder child is chairman of the meeting, an office which is passed on, from week to week, to the person of his or her choice. The office of secretary of the meeting, performed by Irene, a responsible older girl, seemed to be a permanent one. After the meeting Neill gives out pocket money. Bedtimes are according to age, the oldest going at 10:00 o'clock. Adherence to bedtime rules is maintained by 'bedtime officers', who volunteer for this weekly duty.

I have described the daily timetable of Summerhill as the backcloth against which we may consider the school, but in reality it is only its woof; the weft is the personality of its founder and headmaster, A.S. Neill.

It is unfortunate in some respects that Neill's vigorous and idiosyncratic character comes over so strongly from his books, because it allows some critics, otherwise in favour of Summerhill, to say that the school can run due only to the personality of its headmaster. Before my visit, I believed myself that Neill must communicate to the children some indefinable quality which influenced the disciplined running of the school. I now believe that those other visitors, the 1949 H.M.I.s, were nearer the truth when they said that Neill *"has the rare power of being a strong personality without dominating"*. It is not that I wish to question the value of his presence, but it is not the towering presence of an Everest so much as the nine-tenths submergence of an iceberg. Neill is reassuringly there and the landscape of Summerhill, as it is at present, is unimaginable without him, but his main function is that of bulwark against the interference of the grown-up world into his child-haven of freedom. If, from such a short visit, I can assess the regard in which he is held by the children, I should say it is with feeling of deep, if casually expressed, affection.   And although, in the Meeting, other members of the staff were criticised, I cannot recall direct reference to Neill.

On the day following my arrival, Neill asked me if I would take over his lessons for a few days while he went on a lecture tour in the West of England. I agreed and was plunged straight into the life of the school.

Perhaps the thing that will first strike the visitor to Summerhill is the different orientation of the relations between adults and children. These are untrammelled by the usual 'respect' expected by adult dignity from children. Witness to this is the universal and genuinely unselfconscious custom of first names. Thus the headmaster, with a surname so happily ambivalent, is called 'Neill', his wife is 'Ena', the gardener 'Wilf,; the History and Geography master 'Roger', the children 'Zoe', 'Bobby', 'Peter', 'Irene', and so on. There is no insolence at Summerhill because there is no assumed 'dignity'.

To enter into equal relations with a child is a humbling experience - and rather a frightening prospect. Human society has built a little wall of polite and conventional behaviour around each of its members to protect them from other categories; men from women, upper class form lower, and old from young.

Although I had a good book-understanding of, and sympathy with, the ways of Summerhill, I must confess to a certain trepidation at being asked to teach its children - and my first experience was chastening. My first lesson on the day after Neill's departure was attended by twelve of the older children. On the second day five turned up. Happily the younger age groups were less critical.

During the three weeks of my stay, my English lessons alternated between what came to be known as the 'formal' and 'informal.' In the formal I concentrated on G.C.E. material. The informal were spent in etymology, semantics and word study generally. (One of these latter was a study of the morphology of swear-words in polite society. Summerhill must be one of the few schools in England in which this subject could have been treated. As Neill gruffly commented when he saw the chalk-covered blackboard after the lesson, *"They won't get that in the G.C.E."*) Towards the end of my stay, several of the more discriminating children would come to ask me whether I was giving a 'formal' or an 'informal' lesson. The informal ones were quite well-attended, but if I said that the next lesson was to be 'formal', Peter would tell me, without personal feeling, that he would not be coming., but would I tell him when the next informal one was. So much, one is tempted to remark, for the G.C.E.! [Or, thirty years later, one might add, so much for the skill of the teacher.]

While I am writing about my own teaching experience at Summerhill, it may be as well to comment upon the general attitude of the school towards academic education. Although, from time to time, Neill publishes his G.C.E. results in the *Times Educational Supplement* just to show that children not compelled to go to lessons can pass examinations, it is clear to the most casual visitor that there is little danger of academic success ever becoming a fetish in the school. The classrooms are little more than sheds, are drab, uninviting, and, in the colder months, inadequately heated. The books are such as a modern-minded junior school might have cast out 20 years ago, and the equipment seems inadequate. The possible exception is the chemistry laboratory, which is, since the recent retirement of the long-serving chemistry master, no longer used.

There are several reasons for these conditions. Firstly, and quite simply, Summerhill is a poor school, and cannot afford any elaborate teaching equipment; and, besides, the country mansion of a nineteenth century industrial magnate ill-adapts itself to the needs of a residence of study. Secondly, of recent years, the school has been in the doldrums and frequent changes of staff (and these often of third-rate quality) have not made for academic continuity. And the third reason, the most potent, is the headmaster's nihilistic - one is tempted to say, in meaningful pun, "Neillistic" - attitude towards booklearning. When, at a staff meeting, the case of an individual child is discussed, single emphasis is placed on whether he is happy or not, and his attendance or non-attendance at lessons is considered only insofar as it is a symptom of his or her fitting into the school. At one such meeting, Neill remarked *"Duncan is still very polite, and he doesn't seem to be getting any better."*

And if Neill's first concern for the child is happiness it is in no sentimental sense of the word that 'happiness' is sought at Summerhill. Synonymous with 'happy' is the word 'social'. The 'happy' child is the 'social' child.   For, in a community, the individual child must be brought to realise that the happiness of its other members depends on his own sociability, and that he must submit his anti-social actions to the regulation of the community, which happens, in Summerhill, at the weekly Saturday Tribunal.

Homer Lane said of his own meeting in the Little Commonwealth that:

> *"It is in the Citizens' Court that one may get into closer touch with the spirit of the Commonwealth than in any other community function, and it is here that I look for the true spiritual expressions of our boys and girls. "*

He adds:

> *"In the greater community one does not, as a rule, search in the courts for manifestations of the spiritual life of a people, but that is because courts are legal institutions rather than the mouthpiece of a public code of morality as in the Commonwealth."*

Thus it will be seen that such a 'public code of morality' would excite the curiosity of anyone interested in social living, and it will be understood with what anticipation I looked forward to the General Meeting at Summerhill.

What I witnessed was, as I have already led the reader to expect, an unintegrated collection of boys and girls who had little conception of constitutional procedure and, quite simply, did not really know what it was all about.

There are, however, several incidents which may serve to illustrate the pragmatic approach and lack of moral judgement which operate at these meetings. In the first, two of the elder girls (recently arrived at the school) had persistently broken the

bedtime curfew of 10:00 o'clock to go down to the town. Weekly
fines had done nothing to correct them, and at last, after much
discussion, it was decided that they should be exempt from further
fining, so long as they did not make a noise when they came back.
It was argued that this outbreak of persistent anti-sociability was
beyond the control of the community, and that it must wait
patiently till the girls 'got over it' and acquired a sense of
responsibility. And the simple amoral proviso was that they
should not disturb the others when they came in. Nobody
appeared to resent this exception to the rule, and, as far as I could
see, nor did anyone take advantage of its precedence.

Another case is that of Harry, a teenage boy who had become a
thief at Eton. When he was caught, his crime served as text for a
moral lecture delivered to the assembled school, before whom he
was then beaten. He was subsequently expelled.

Shortly after his arrival at Summerhill he began to steal again,
and, in the course of time, a young plaintiff at the meeting
accused him of stealing a fountain pen. Several others witnessed
having seen Harry with the pen, and the meeting's chairman
required him to return it. The general vote levied a small fine on
him, and passed on to the next business. No more was said, and
Harry attested to me his deep astonishment that after the meeting
no one made any reference to his delinquency, and people asked
him to dance in the usual way at the customary Saturday night
festivities.

Besides the General Meeting, there is the 'Special' meeting. This
is convened by anyone who considers that the nature of his
complaint is too urgent to wait till Saturday. One of these is
especially worthwhile recording. It was during Neill's absence.
When the school had gathered, the chairman formally asked who
had called the special meeting. Ena said that she had. She then
spoke briefly, with few marks of emphasis, and totally without
personal rancour. She had heard one of the boys making an
insulting reference to the colour of a negro girl's skin. She said
that Summerhill had always been a place where individuality had
been encouraged; and that racial, political and religious tolerance
had always been fostered, and she deplored any sign of the colour
bar in the school. Since the person concerned had not been long

at Summerhill she did not wish to prosecute or even name him, but hoped that nothing further would need to be said about the matter. The children listened throughout in silence, and little reference was made to the meeting afterwards.

Another meeting occurred towards the end of my visit to Summerhill. This was called a 'Special, Special Meeting', and was, as far as I know, unique in the history of the school. Neill had been increasingly worried about the unhappy state of the school, and he called the pupils and teachers together to talk about it. They met, not in the hall, but in the more comfortable staff sitting-room. I noticed that several of the elder children were not present. They told me afterwards that they were tired of the anti-sociability and that they had no faith in discussion as a remedy. The meeting lasted about an hour, little was concluded, but grievances were freely aired, and, as Neill sat quietly smoking his pipe, saying little, this may have been all he had hoped for.

From the point of view of the reader of this essay, however, one item of interest may have arisen form this meeting: my credentials as a commentator on Summerhill. I had stayed silent, and at one juncture in the discussion, Peter Wood asked if the meeting might have the benefit of the opinion of a visitor - myself. Most of the children looked about them, and through me, in surprise, and there were several exclamations of "What visitor!"

Whether such a complete and unnoticed absorption into the community qualifies or disqualifies me to comment on Summerhill will depend upon the attitude of the reader, but I propose to conclude this chapter by giving my overall impressions of the school, for what they are worth.

Summerhill is not - save in the deepest etymological sense - a school; it is rather an 'unschool', where the usual educational values are upturned, apparently merely perversely. But, in fact, Summerhill only re-orientates priorities. The child is its priority. The conventional school's priorities of adult authority, decorous behaviour, and academocentrism must at Summerhill yield to the child.

Press coverage of the school has tended towards an emphasis on sensationalism, on swearing, smoking, and 'kissing in the open'. Since I regard 'swearing' as nothing more than a tribal code of taboo-words, of little importance, my opinion may be invalid in some quarters, but I can only comment that the free use of swear-words seemed to rob them of their offensiveness, and certainly reinstated many useful anatomical and functional words which our day-to-day language lacks.

Smoking is allowed at Summerhill in the belief that if one is allowed to do something long enough one will grow out of it. From the premises of my short visit, I obviously cannot comment on the effectiveness of this method. Most of the older children smoked, as did nearly all the staff.

During my three weeks at Summerhill I did not see any 'kissing in the open', and, although I may be ingenuous, such heterosexual friendships as existed were conducted with restraint and without lack of dignity.

So distorted has the image of Summerhill become by the sensation-seeking press that, as one who has been able to acquire a broader perspective of what the school it trying to do by living in it for a while, I would like to state, in conclusion, that I consider Summerhill to be a community where the sane priorities of social living are implicit in its daily life. Far from considering Neill an extremist - much less a crank - I regard him as a middle-of-the-roader, whose presence in a saner world might well have passed unnoticed, but whose published findings of his little educational laboratory in East Suffolk may contribute to the understanding of the proper basis of psychological health in our schools of the future.

My visit to Summerhill at an end, I left by the front gate, beside which stood the wall whereon was written the inscription which not only identifies the school, but, with a warning to motorists, accidentally defines its ethos:

SUMMERHILL - CHILDREN PLAYING.

Chapter nine

Summerhill re-visited, 1961

Summerhill is a most congenial place to re-visit. There is a refreshing lack of formality in greeting Summerhillians, both child and adult, after a few months' interval. This was a flying visit during which I recorded no new impressions.

Before I left Summerhill last time, Neill asked me if I knew anyone who wanted a job as a gardener, whose main qualifications would be adaptability and a liking for children. I replied that I had a friend, at present working in an office, whom I considered ideal for the school. His name was Wilf, and he had spent some five years travelling about the Continent, working at a variety of jobs: farm-hand in France, butcher's-boy in Geneva, telephone-operator in Seville, and factory worker in Hanover, among others. He had studied French, German, Spanish, and Italian, spoke them colloquially, and had read into the respective literatures. Neill's suspicious comment was, 'Is he an intellectual?'

Wilf did go to Summerhill as the gardener (wages £5 a week, the same as the teachers), and I give a selection from his letters, which supplement my own rather fragmentary impressions. This selection has been made as an afterthought, and I asked Wilf's permission to reproduce it only after the last letter had reached me. The quotations are roughly chronological.

(The letter following the interview.) December 1961 Durham

Dear Bryn,.
As you prophesied, I liked the atmosphere of [Summerhill] very much and was very impressed by the old man and his wife Ena. Consequently I've arranged to give up my job in the Civil Service and start at Summerhill at the beginning of next term, on January 18th.

Saturday evening [Jan 20] The Meeting has finished, the gram is blaring out a rock'n roll number, and already I feel part of Summerhill as I sit in the staff-room writing this letter.

You were right when you said that this was real education. I've never seen a bunch of kids more natural and uninhibited as these are. Their frankness is wonderful to observe ... It's a little sad too, to think that so few children are given this chance of self-expression and that the majority must spend their life governed as it is by a repressive environment.

Wilf uses several of the words common to the supporters of the progressive educational movement, and I think it ought to be explained that he had never heard of Summerhill or any other similar school at the beginning of December, and his impressions are those of one who views the school with unprejudiced eyes.

January 27, 1962
Tonight's Meeting was mostly taken up with bullying ... x y, and z being accused in a general sort of way ... Visits from American professors ... Financial help coming from Unitarians in America ... Most kids going to lessons.

[undated. Probably early March]
There seems to be a different atmosphere in the school since half-term. The kids are welding together, and fellows like x, y, and z are not in their usual destructive mood.

Are you interested in my observations after spending a term at Summerhill? I'm rather perturbed at the behaviour of the old pupils who came down at the end of the term. They are a really decent lot but without exception they all trooped off to the pub and quite a few of them came back having drunk too much...

There's a lack of culture in the school. And I think that we, the staff, are at fault. We don't communicate with the children, especially the older ones, to the necessary degree. I think that kids like Zoe, Irene, and Al would benefit from literature which would make them think more deeply. These same kids seem sensitive and intelligent and likely to find happiness in life, but at the moment they seem to be stagnating mentally...

We don't know enough about child psychology, and I include Neill. We have problems with the children and we just have no idea how to cope with them. ... The kids are wonderful. I've never met kids as sincere, as loving and as well-balanced (integrated) as our kids are. For all its shortcomings the school is doing a wonderful job and this sort of education must be the education of the future or at least the basis of future education. We need a good public relations man... .

Irene told me that a crowd of them went to the local church last Easter. When I asked her if any of them went back, she replied, 'What! And listen to somebody standing in a box frightening everybody with death and destruction! Not on your life! I want to be happy ...' Talking of an ex-pupil, Olly said: 'He was a homosexual and religious. God! I didn't mind his being homosexual... but religious!'

[Drop in frequency of letters. No date.]
The summer term has opened very quietly indeed, and it appears as though the kids are really forming themselves into a community now. We've had no instances of bullying so far and there is a very happy and healthy feeling throughout the school. The greatest news I can retail is that David has started to attend lessons and is very keen in every lesson he applies himself to. As Neill says, he seems to have finally 'turned the corner.' ... Other news of great import is that Johnny too is attending lessons and is just as keen as David. This is simply terrific! Actually of all the kids that I would term 'eligible' for lessons, only Paul, Lawrence, and Li don't attend. Peter is another, but he is engaged in business affairs: he is an agent for an American coin-dealer and is really going great guns. A few weeks ago he took part in a radio interview and this very evening we've all been watching him being interviewed on TV. He was so natural that it was a joy to see him on the screen.

In this letter Wilf mentions that he had been accepted as an Associate of the Institute of Linguists in the Spanish language. He must surely be one of the most highly qualified gardeners in the country.

Summerhill Revisited: June 8th to the 17th 1962.

Summerhill's most agreeable season is the summer. Or perhaps it was just the changed atmosphere of the school. In the account of A Visitor to Summerhill I made no reference to individual children, because I thought that I would be working from insufficient evidence. Now I feel in a good enough position to record the case-histories of three children who I observed in the visits I made over the period of twelve months.

Stephen a boy of about 14, arrived at Summerhill a few days before my first week-end visit in May, 1961. I noticed him sitting by himself with his head hanging and his shoulders hunched. He spoke to no one, and once I saw him furtively tormenting a four year old boy by taking away his tricycle.

On Sunday evening Neill tells a story to the younger children which he makes up as he goes along, introducing the names of the real children listening to him into the imaginary tale to give it first hand interest. On this particular evening, the story was about a school in Suffolk where headmaster, a man called Neill, was so old and so silly that he was asked to retire in favour of a Mr Buggins. Mr Buggins, when he arrived, said that he wanted to make Summerhill a good school, where the children must go to lessons and respect their teachers. If children did not do as they were told they would be caned. Soon a resistance movement grew up among the pupils which culminated in Mr Buggins' ignominious flight from the school. The story was a piece of whimsy which the children vastly enjoyed, crying out when they were mentioned personally and laughing when Buggins was outwitted.

But most interesting were Stephen's reactions. He was the only one of the older ones there, and had probably drifted in with the others because of his unfamiliarity with the school's routine. He sat listening to the early development of the story without emotion. But when Mr Buggins, who for him represented Authority, was defied he looked up with interest. When he was tricked, he giggled and laughed. At one point, when Buggins was outwitted in a particularly humiliating way, Stephen rolled about helplessly on the sofa, clawing the leather covering with his hands and shrieking with such uncontrollably hysterical laughter that Neill had to stop talking and the other called on him to shut up.

On my second longer visit I hardly noticed Stephen. He came to no lessons at all, much less to mine, he never spoke to me, and did not encourage the friendly advances which I made to him in casual contact. He was not a popular boy, had no special friends, and was often the butt of the others' jokes. I retain one impression on one such occasion, when one of the older boys was teasing him. He made no reply, just grinned uneasily and moved away. But it seemed to me that his head was held just a little higher.

I should perhaps not have noticed such a minute sign of change of temper, and certainly not have recorded it here, but for the striking alteration I saw in the boy on my third visit, four months later.

When I arrived, I contacted Wilf, and, in the course of his daily duties, we went to mix the chicken food. While we were so employed, Stephen came in, and, seeing Wilf, he shouted some insulting joke at him and playfully charged him with his shoulder. Wilf, accustomed to the joke, stood his ground and gave as good as he got. The boy continued to abuse him, now obscenely, and now in imitation of Wilf's northern brogue. Wilf continued to mix the chicken food placidly, retorting in imitation of Stephen's Southern brogue. After 10 minutes spent in playful badinage, Stephen went off.

Where possible in this essay I have eschewed personal opinion, but so strong was the impression that Stephen's change made on me that I think it worth recording. When I first saw him, in May '61, his face was dull, expressionless and incurious. In February '62, his behaviour was infantile, but his countenance bore the marked signs of an 'awakening', both mental and emotional. It was alive and alert, and the carriage of his body was more erect and confident. Had I only photographic evidence of these two Stephens, the rest of my essay were superfluous.

When I next saw Stephen in June, he no longer felt the need to annoy adults, had joined a small gang of boys slightly younger than himself, and appeared to be well integrated into the school. I had my first personal contact with the boy on this visit. We had several games of chess together at his instance.

I first met Joanie in October 1961. She was a little girl of six who had arrived only a few weeks before. She was pretty, petite, impeccably dressed, well-groomed, and her manners were charming.

When I saw her the following February there was as striking a transformation in Joanie as I had observed in Stephen - in reverse. Her clothes were untidy, her face smudged, her hands grubby, her hair unkempt, and there was a marked alteration in her manner. She pouted often, demanded piggyback rides, and either sulked if refused, or became even more importunate if her desires were complied with. I witnessed a game of Happy Families in which she was on the way to losing. She accused the other players of cheating, flung her remaining cards on the ground, and stormed out of the room.

I was greatly looking forward to seeing her on my next visit, to observe the next stage in her behaviour cycle, but, unfortunately, she was visiting her parents. As it stands, this is a cautionary tale about what happens to a child who attends Summerhill.

In each of the case histories which I have recounted the behaviour pattern is well-defined and easy to follow. Stephen came from a repressive environment, where his actions and thoughts were very much dictated by authority. Before he could become self-respecting he had to mock-rebel against the adults at Summerhill - in the incident I have described, against Wilf. Joanie came from a background which required an unnatural politeness in her. A few months of freedom revealed the real child. A few more months might have shown us that child socialised.

The third case which I have to recount is a much more complex one. Marla, newly arrived at Summerhill, was an American 13-year-old, who had been brought up in a consciously progressive family. There was no taboo on nakedness, she was permitted to swear, she was told that school lessons were not important, and her attitude was non-religious. While she was not in the least overtly anti-social, she was, at the same time one of the most uncomfortable children to deal with in the school. She was 'blasé', pert and unresponsive. As she came to my lessons, I knew her quite well, but she was not a child whom I looked forward to seeing again on my visits to Summerhill.

Great was my surprise, then, when I saw Marla in the following June. It was a much more open-faced child who shouted a friendly greeting to me from an upstairs window when I arrived. Her manner was more outgoing, friendly and natural, and she no longer wandered about in aloof isolation, but had joined a group of girls of her own age.

Marla is the apparently contradictory case of a child who was brought up in a consciously progressive atmosphere, and yet who only found herself in the freedom of Summerhill. We will find the answer, I think, in the word 'conscious' - consciously progressive. It is just as harmful to the child's individuality to mould her or his mind into the contours of 'progressive' ideas as it is to mould it in the light of a repressive morality. As parents and teachers, holding views however enlightened, we must trust the child, in the meaningful idiom, 'to make up her or his own mind', not only in particular decisions, but in her or his general outlook on life.

Wilf's last letter contained encouraging news for the sympathisers of Summerhill:
[Early October, 1962] Things are cracking here. Twenty-two new kids this term and the school is prospering. The kids seem a good bunch and are fitting into the school. We are fortunate in that one or two older kids are good types and steady the others.

Summerhill Revisited: July 1963

A visit of three days. The conduct of the Meeting was much more orderly. But what impressed me most was the considerable diminution of noise, and increase of orderliness at mealtimes. I had come to accept the oppressive noise of raucous talking and shouting as a necessary, if unfortunate, concomitant to education-free children. The tables were also cleared of dirty plates spontaneously and orderly, although this may, of course, have been due only to a recent campaign.

Chapter ten

The Summerhill idea

"What cannot be doubted is that a piece of fascinating and valuable educational research is going on here which it would do all educationalists good to see."

HMI Report 1949

"How can we have happy homes with love in them when the home is a tiny corner of a homeland that shows hate socially in a hundred ways? You can see why I cannot look upon education as a matter of exams and classes and learning. The school evades the basic issue: all the Greek and Maths and History in the world will not help to make the home more loving, the child free from inhibitions, the parent free from neurosis...

"The future of Summerhill itself may be of little import. But the Summerhill idea is of the greatest importance to humanity. New generations must be given the chance to grow in freedom. The bestowal of freedom is the bestowal of love. And only love can save the world. "

A.S.Neill

In his classic work on the philosophy of education Sir Percy Nunn contributes to our understanding of a people's culture, by defining two words: 'hormic' and 'mnemic'. It is not only by our hormic selves, or instinctual energies, but by our mnemic selves, or the traditions and culture which are transmitted from generation to generation, that we grow in knowledge and develop in mind and spirit over the ages.

The stepping stones on which men and societies rise to higher things are never their dead selves, but their mnemic selves, alive and actively growing. It is indeed true that our traditional culture nourishes our psychological and spiritual development, but it is no less true that forcible inculcation - 'teaching' - of the outworn beliefs and customs of one generation may stultify the growth of the next.

In the words of Richard Jefferies:

> "... We die through our ancestors; we are murdered by our ancestors. Their dead hands stretch forth from the tomb and drag us down to their mouldering bones. We in our turn are now at this moment preparing death for our unborn posterity."

Jefferies (1848-87) lived during a century and in a country in which many were finding it imperative so exorcise the ghosts of their 'murdering ancestors', and painfully reject their old inhibiting beliefs. But it was not only in England that the louring spiritual climate was forcing many to abandon their thought-abodes of tribal faith.   Frustrated by the narrow Norwegian community in which he lived, there was one who dared to raise his voice against *"the pillars of society"*. One of Ibsen's plays was *Ghosts*, in which he tried to analyse the harmfulness of tribal belief to society.   The most penetrating passage in the play - in Ibsen, perhaps - is the one in which Mrs Alving talks to the local parson, the representative of the community's religion:

> "I almost think we're all of us ghosts, Pastor Manders. It's not only what we have inherited from our father and mother that 'walks' in us. It's all sorts of dead ideas, and lifeless old beliefs, and so forth. They have no vitality, but they cling to us all the same, and we can't get rid of them. Whenever I take up a newspaper, I seem to see Ghosts gliding between the lines. There must be Ghosts all the country over, as thick as the sand of the sea. And then we are, one and all, so pitifully afraid of the light."

This problem of 'ghosts', related elsewhere in this essay to 'the emotional plague', seems particularly incident upon the state of man's communal growth, known as 'civilisation'. Certainly we can perceive its symptoms in one of the first civilisations known to mankind, the China of 2,500 years ago. Lao Tzu, poet and philosopher, found much to criticise in the increasingly bureaucratic and regimented way in which the state was governing the people's lives, and he dreamt of a time when government might have as its first concern the happiness of the common people, and not power over them. He held, in terms remarkably coincident with those used by Ibsen, over 2,000 years later, that if people were not interfered with, they would not suffer outworn beliefs to harm them, and would derive only what was beneficial to them from the traditions of their forefathers:

"If you manage people by letting them alone,
Ghosts of the dead shall not haunt you.
Not that there are not ghosts
But that their influence becomes propitious
In the sound existence of a living man."

But we must not be permitted to talk glibly of 'the people'. It is the formative years of *childhood* that determine what the next adult generation is to become. Parents, and those who have charge of children, must nourish the child's individual and societal development, and avoid stifling with an outworn code of morality.

As Kahil Gibran, the Persian poet, warns us:

"Your children are not your children.
They are the sons and daughters of Life's longing for itself.
They come through you but not from you,
And though they are with you yet they belong not to you.
You may give them your love but not your thoughts,
For they have their own thoughts.
You may have their bodies but not their souls,
For their souls dwell in the house of tomorrow,
Which you cannot visit, not even in your dreams.
You may strive to be like them, but seek not to make them like you.
For life goes not backward nor tarries with yesterday."

Such parents may be found, as we have seen else where, in the Trobriand Islands [1] *Sex and Repression in Savage Society*, by Branislaw Malinowski, in the Marquesan Islands [2], *Typee*, by

Herman Melville, and among the wandering Eskimo tribes [3], *People of the Deer*, by Farley Mowat, but the parents of our civilisation find the pressures of convention and social taboo distract them from an unqualified approving love.

The authority with which the parent invests himself in order to ensure the forcible continuance of the old beliefs gives rise to a smouldering resentment in the growing child, which, if he has any spirit, will break fire in adolescence. The university student may find outlet in 'rags', in childish jokes and other high-spirited ways of making up for his frustrated childhood. Many children may have to join gangs who mark this initiation into manhood by acts of hooliganism. (A case history of such a growing boy, which had a profound influence on the young Allie Neill, and described as "a masterpiece" by J.B.Priestley, is *The House with the Green Shutters* by George Douglas).

But most people, having made their gesture of teenage revolt, settle down and assume the role towards *their* children against which they had so lately rebelled in their elders. There are a few, however, who do not forget the suffering of their youth, and continue to attack the injustices which caused them. One such is the American writer, Henry Miller. In his study of Arthur Rimbaud, Miller gives us valuable insight into the problem of adolescent rebellion. Rimbaud was, of course, the French poet whose life as a child was exemplary both in his behaviour and his school work, but who, at the age of 14, made a complete moral volte face, ran away from home, became dissolute in his habits, and, in his poetry, fiercely denounced the institutions of his day.

In Miller's words:

> *"He saw that science had become as great a hoax as religion, that nationalism was a farce, patriotism a fraud, education a form of leprosy, and that morals were for cannibals. With every piercing shaft he hit the bull's eye. No one had keener vision, truer aim, than the golden-haired boy of seventeen with the periwinkle blue eyes."*

But for Miller, Rimbaud was important not only as a poet and visionary.

"I like to think of him as the Columbus of Youth, as the one who extended the boundaries of that only partially explored domain. Youth ends where manhood begins, it is said. A phrase without meaning, since from the beginning of history man has never enjoyed the full measure of youth nor known the limitless possibilities of adulthood. How can one know the splendour and fullness of youth if one's energies are consumed in combatting the errors and falsities of parents and ancestors? Is youth to waste its strength unlocking the grip of death? Is youth's only mission on earth to rebel, to destroy, to assassinate? What are the dreams of youth? Are they always to be regarded as follies? Are they to be populated only with chimeras? Dreams are the shoots and buds of the imagination: they have the right the lead pure lives also. Stifle or deform youth's dreams and you destroy the creator. Where there has been no real youth there can be no real manhood. If society has come to resemble a collection of deformities, is it not the work of our educators and preceptors?"

But how many of our *"educators and preceptors"* are capable of understanding the nature of the work to be done? Are not many teachers merely the hod-carriers of education, who accept the mores of their tribe or nation as unquestioningly as any other professional?

The architects of enlightened educational theory are the minority, like, Percy Nunn:

"There are no eternal moral principles which men 'ought' to follow; what we 'ought' to do now is not what our grandfathers 'ought' to have done, for our world is not theirs. The morality of an industrial age, with vast concentrations of populations, complex communications and immense technical powers, cannot be the same as that of one of the old simple communities."

This doctrine has evidently a most direct and drastic bearing on educational theory. Instead of seeking to preserve the 'culture' of the past, it should concentrate upon the present, and aim constantly at fostering in boys and girls at school the experimental attitude towards its material, economic, hygienic and moral problems - teaching them to realise that these cannot be separated, but are all aspects of the one great problem of increasing welfare of mankind.

But this minority, whose members preoccupy themselves with 'the welfare of mankind' is rare indeed. Are they so rare that there are not enough like-minded people of the same generation to perceive their greatness, and they are recognised only posthumously?

Often they are not concerned so much with the moral principles underlying their causes as passionately inflamed against some immediate social injustice which stirs their conscience, and impels them to devote their whole life to redressing it.

John Stuart Mill writes about the broader cause of freedom:

> *"In general, those who have been in advance of society in thought and feeling have left [the issue of individual liberty] unassailed in principle, however they may have come into conflict with it in some of its details. They have occupied themselves rather in enquiring what things society ought to like or dislike, than in questioning whether its likings or dislikings should be a law to individuals. They preferred endeavouring to alter the feelings of mankind on the particular points on which they were themselves heretical, rather than make common cause in defense of freedom, with heretics generally."*

One heretic who **does** *"make common cause in defense of freedom"* is the twentieth century educator, A.S.Neill. His premises are not, however, constitutional, but psychological. His careful observation of the child has taught him that much of our conventional way of treating the child, both at home and in school, is pernicious, and inhibits to his full mental and emotional growth. His heresy attacks the Church for its flesh-hating doctrines which teach the child a sense of sin; it attacks the schools for their unimaginative and authoritarian methods of instruction; and it attacks the whole of society for refusing to allow the child to grow emotionally.

Neill wrote books about his findings for over fifty years, and, in certain circles, is internationally recognised as an educational philosopher. Why then are not people convinced by the apparently demonstrable truth of his theories, and impelled to do something about it? Bernard Shaw provides an answer:

> "The Machine [our 'Establishment'] will not let them. Always the Machine... In short , they do not know. They try to reform Society as an old lady might try to restore a broken-down locomotive by prodding it with a knitting needle. And this is not because they are born fools, but because they have been educated, not into manhood and freedom, but into blindness and slavery by the parents and schoolmasters, themselves the victims of a similar misdirection, and consequently of The Machine. They do not want liberty. They have not been educated to want it. They choose slavery and inequality; and all the other evils are automatically added to them."

Thus it is clear that the putting into practice of Neill's theories would endanger the intellectual vested interests of, among others, the teaching profession, who, while they are prepared to acknowledge that they have learnt much from the progressive education movement, are no more willing than the previous generations of teachers to admit that they have anything *further* to learn from it.

Ibsen's Dr Stockmann arraigns the collected townspeople for their narrowness and cowardice:

> "The worst enemy of truth and freedom in our society is the compact majority. Yes, the damned, compact liberal majority. The liberal majority. That is to say, the educated majority. "

The *liberal* majority, the educated majority; applied to the teaching profession, the blinkered majority who have been taught a method of instruction but who cannot see the wider issues outside their narrow professionalism.

An early interest of the young Dottoressa Montessori was that of educating sub-normal children. Her signal success encouraged her to apply her methods to normal, intelligent children, with such effect that the influence of her educational theories is now world-wide.

Neill's early experience was with emotionally unstable 'problem' children. In later years, when his reputation had grown, he was able to reject the 'problems' and accept only children from normal, happy homes. Like Montessori with her mentally-handicapped pupils, Neill found that his psychological methods worked with tenfold success upon children without emotional disorders, compared with his achievements with delinquents. Prevention, however, is better than cure.

Neill's theories about the treatment of juvenile delinquency are nowadays unexceptional. Homer Lane is honoured, David Wills was subsidised by the state, Otto Shaw and Mr Lyward were both respected by most advanced, thinking people concerned with crime in young children and adolescents.

Neill is ridiculed because he argues that what will cure a disordered psyche will augment the living strength of a healthy one. Although we may agree that this sort of treatment may be all right for a 'certain type of child' - the delinquent - yet we strenuously reject any suggestion that it is right for normal children, *our* children.

As a writer on juvenile delinquency Neill has already secured an honourable reputation. Only the future will show how far he has the right to be regarded as an educator - in the deepest sense of the word - or even, what every real educator must be, a social reformer. What, in short, is the future of 'The Summerhill Idea'? Whatever Neill's contribution to it, it is certain that, given conducive circumstances, 'The Summerhill Idea' in social, moral, and educational fields will fulfil itself over the centuries. To claim this is to stretch the phrase beyond reasonable definition.

Summerhill is a school, and we must find some criterion whereby
it may be judged, some definition of the purpose of education.
Krishnamurti gives us one:

> *"Education should help us to discover lasting values so
> that we do not merely cling to formulas or repeat slogans;
> it should help us to break down our national and social
> barriers, instead of emphasising them, for they breed
> antagonism between man and man. Unfortunately, the
> present system of education is making us subservient,
> mechanical, and deeply thoughtless; though it awakens us
> intellectually, inwardly it leaves us incomplete, stultified
> and uncreative."*

Neill, despite the apparent assertiveness of his books, would have
been the last to claim, in personal conversation, infallibility for
his ideas or for his school. If one may hazard a guess into the
future, to a time many years after his death, when his theories will
be exhumed and he is canonized into the educational calendar,
one might conjecture that Neill's opinions about sex and religion,
while in the main sane for their time, will be considered to have
been largely coloured, that is, tainted, by his own puritanical
upbringing and a too eager and uncritical acceptance of the
Freudian theory of psychoanalysis which will, let it be
remembered, itself be superseded.

His contribution to the theory of learning will pass unnoticed,
because students 'of a future age' will not understand the purging
effect of Neill's fulminations against 'education in the head'. The
educational historian may criticize him for throwing out the baby
with the bath-water, for throwing out, in his hatred of
head-education, all benefits of booklearning. Neill might answer
that he preferred a dirty, but healthy, baby to one enervated by the
too sterile academocentrism of our educational theory.

So, to resume, whatever may be the shortcomings of the school,
whether due to the outlook of its headmaster or to the difficulties,
financial or otherwise, inherent in ploughing a lone and rebellious
furrow, Summerhill answers Krishnamurti's requirement that
"education should... discover lasting values" and *"break down
our national and social barriers instead of emphasising them"*;

and, *speaking generally*, and even taking into account many notable advances, our present educational system must plead 'guilty' to a charge of, *"making us subservient, mechanical, and deeply thoughtless."*

The Summerhill Idea, then, is, in a few words - Neill's, of course:

> *"the bestowal of freedom. and the bestowal of freedom is the bestowal of love. And only love can save the world."*

Let Krishnamurti take up the words:

> *"Only love can bring about the understanding of another. Where there is love there is instantaneous communion with the other, on the same level and at the same time. It is because we ourselves are so dry, empty and without love that we have allowed governments and systems to take over the education of our children and the direction of our lives; but governments want efficient technicians, not human beings, because human beings become dangerous to governments and to organized religions as well. That is why governments and religious organizations seek to control education."*

So, if we wish to rescue the human race from the polarizing and depersonalising maw of the State and of State education, we must have recourse to what has been so inadequately and amorphously defined in these pages as the Summerhill Idea. Neill would not claim the single authorship of the idea. It is the purpose of this essay to suggest that instead of being a 'crank school', a mere vagary of a too permissive educational system, Summerhill lies at the heart of a more humane and enlightened movement for tackling societal, moral and educational problems.

But speculation about some possible future utopia can degenerate into mere dilettantism. Neill's discoveries can teach us something about our most pressing, current socio-political problem: war.

The United Nations Charter reads:

> *"Since wars begin in the minds of men it is in the minds of men that the defences of peace must be constructed."*

Modern psychology has taught us of the retributive effects of repression on the psyche. When natural human impulses are inhibited, they are not eliminated, as is intended, but driven underground into the unconscious, whence they re-emerge as anti-social behaviour in the individual. Anti-social behaviour is multiplied a millionfold when a whole culture is repressive, and, whatever the political precipitating factors, mass anti-sociability, or war, is the result.

Anthropologists like Malinowski and Margaret Mead have studied non-repressive cultures and recorded the full, happy, and social development of free children, free from neurosis, into complete, balanced adults.

May we adapt by one word the Charter?

> *"Since wars begin in the minds of* children *it is in the minds of* children *that the defences of peace must be constructed."*

H.G.Wells describes in his autobiography the military fantasies of his adolescence ('my Hitler stage'), and relates them to the growing Nazi movements in Germany (written in 1936):

> *"Adolf Hitler is nothing more than one of my 13-year-old reveries come true. A whole generation of Germans has failed to grow up."*

Elsewhere Wells says that the survival of homo sapiens depends upon the result of the race between education and catastrophe. This is true, but we must re-define and expand the word 'education'. Our present understanding of it is narrowly professional and pusillanimous.

Writing in 1944 about the deeper causes of the problem of war and the part that education must play in its solution, A.S.Neill says:

> *"It is the unexpressed unconscious of humanity that has made this bloody war, and all our university graduates and school subjects have been powerless to prevent it. War is inevitable if humanity expresses its anger and hate, if its*

emotional life has been neglected and kept down.   The emotion behind a 'Heil Hitler!' is a force that overwhelms all the mere intellectualism in Germany.   Emotion rules the world, and, as our emotions are largely bottled up, emotion tends to destroy the world.   So that the real problem is: 'What can we do to educate humanity so that this emotion is not bottled up?' In our small way we at Summerhill try to give this education."

chapter eleven

One man's practice: Summerhill unvisited (1962 - 1996)

For over thirty years I did not visit Summerhill. I was too busy running schools of my own. The foregoing essay, with minor recension and updating, was written at a college of education in the early '60's - under the aegis of a Social Studies Department, not of Education, of course. Neill read it, corrected it, and suggested that I send it to his publishers, so it may be taken to represent his own understanding of his life's work. I see now that it was less a study of Neill himself than a exercise in locating 'The Summerhill Idea', the co-ordinates of students of the principles of Freedom, Democracy, and the Ethics of the human condition.

I essayed some research into ex-Summerhillians, and into the opinions of contemporary experts in the broad field of education: among others, a philosopher, a psychologist and a poet, (Bertrand Russell, Cyril Burt and Charles Causley).

I was particularly interested in researching how theory can translate into practice. As editor of the Summerhill magazine in the late '60s, I invited exponents of 'The Summerhill Idea', including John Aitkenhead, R.F.Mckenzie and Michael Duane to contribute articles.

Shortly afterwards, I was appointed to my first headship. Now the circumstances of my life permitted me to essay - and assay - the principles of 'The Summerhill Idea' myself.   Of course, Neill cannot be held responsible for the practice of his theory, which had to be modified, in any case, by the different circumstances in which I found myself.   Also it must be affirmed that my enthusiasm for his ideas has never, early or late, made me other than a pragmatic rather than a doctrinaire practitioner: if a theory had not 'worked', I would have abandoned it.

The terms of reference of this first school which my wife Meg and I opened and ran for seven years could not have been more contrary, on every count, to our model for an unschool.

On the one hand, Summerhill was an independent, rural, boarding school supported by fee-paying parents who chose it for highly esoteric ideological reasons.

On the other, our small day school was sponsored by a Local Authority in a city, providing respite care for behaviourally disordered children mostly on free school dinners, whose parents had never heard of Summerhill.

Summerhillism in a state school? In a day school? Would it work? Could it work? What happens when, in Blishen's phrase, one lets 'run wild' children already clinically defined as 'wild'? (I define and differentiate here several terms: 'Summerhillian' to refer to Summerhill the school and all that pertains to it; 'summerhillism' and 'summerhillist' to refer to The SummerhillI Idea; and 'summerhillery' to refer to the trappings, what I shall describe as the 'kindling sticks' of the Idea.)

With all the confidence of inexperience, I installed the elements of the Summerhill Idea in their full contradictoriness:

- the new school had no religious assembly; staff and pupils convened daily in an hour-long meeting in which behavioural and ethical issues were discussed;

- the new school encouraged each child to attend class, but permitted him, quite dispassionately, not to.

- the new school disavowed both punitivism and permissivism. It 'punished' no child; nor did it 'let him off'. It confronted him, moreover, with personal responsibility, and taxed him with restitution.

- there was mutual first-naming of child and adult, including the occasional visiting police officer.

So the kindling sticks of The Summerhill Idea, of 'Democracy' were assembled and laid carefully one across another. Two Cheers! Now let us await the flame of Love in the Beloved Republic to ignite and suffuse our community with its warmth.

The Meeting into 'Moot'

Summerhill's Meeting was held every Saturday evening, before the handing out of pocket money and the weekly dance. We convened our 'Moot' each morning, just like any other 'Assembly' in the land. Our community's forum, however, was addressed specifically to the manifestly irresponsible and occasionally violent behaviour of its members.

August Aichhorn's Dantesque account of his experiment in post-World-War Austria had prepared us for the first grim months. We had to ride out the sudden squalls of quarrelling and the storms of exploding distress and anger of these deeply emotionally disturbed children.

We 'approved' the child for month after month, before beginning the painful operation of non-recriminative probing and cauterising the areas of emotional disturbance evidenced by his unbehaviour. The daymares continued as the cogs of the Moot scraped, clanked, and shrilled oillessly. So this is what it is like when 'wild' children 'run wild'.

In a day school for children from mostly disadvantaged backgrounds, we could not employ 'fining', time-honoured since 1914 by Homer Lane in his Little Commonwealth. We had to devise a 'restitution' for each 'misdemeanour' - a 'punishment' for each 'crime'. Thus our policy, in this respect, owed more to W.S.Gilbert than to A.S.Neill.

Our intention most sublime was not to punish, and each succeeding day, week, month, brought less shouting, less wrangling; more rationality, more humour. The character of the

Moot changed from a judicial 'court' to an exercise of conviviality, a daily conversation between friends.

The Option to Attend the Classroom

The child has a right not to be coerced to attend class. Child-rights aside, it is simply miseducative to force-feed academically. Like religious belief, learning is too important to be made compulsory. Learning is an appetite. To be taught well is a privilege. There is, however, something inimical in the child-mind, the older it gets, to being 'made' to learn.

I do not treat of absolutes such as 'Freedom'; I prefer to think of the 'option', in which there is some sense of commitment by the child. 'Commitment' in this sense, includes for the summerhillist, of course, the commitment not to attend class.

Most teachers who have laboured in the vineyard of compulsory class may persuade themselves in the end that if such assiduity achieve so little, they must not let up - in the time-honoured words of the Termly Report, they 'must work harder'.

What, then, does happen when the classroom is made voluntary? Quantitatively, not a lot. There are variables, of course, between the different ages, and, in my specialism, the degrees of behavioural disorder and of clinical school phobism in the individual child. In short, the answer to my question is that, offered the choice, most children attend class for most of the time. (One of our pupils, studying for her 'A' level Maths, did research the point once for me over several months, supervised by her teacher, and the result, probably distorted by 25% of school phobics at the time, was an 82% attendance.)

Qualitatively, there are significant differences in the voluntary classroom. Firstly, the atmosphere is more conducive to study, both individually and as a group. Secondly, there are few 'discipline' problems, simply because a child would not be present if he does not wish to study.

In such cases of 'indiscipline', to which my specialism is prone, the child's right to attend class is first challenged by the teacher,

then, in rare persistent cases, withdrawn temporarily: aut disce,
aut discede. The teacher has rights too.

So much for the application of summerhillism within the school.
I was also faced with several dilemmas outside the parameters of
the school premises, demonised by Neill in book-titles such as *The
Problem Parent* and *The Problem Teacher.*

The 'Problem' Parent

We knew, did we not, that the 'Problem' Parent was the cause of
The Problem Child, was, indeed, 'to blame'? If only she or he
would treat the child in a more enlightened way, there would be
no problem. So, the posited solution is to get the child away from
the parent.

In the day situation in which we found ourselves, the 'problem
child' and the 'problem parent' continued to co-habit, and we had
to include this factor in the equation of our problem-solving.
Indeed, we met several of these 'demons', first casually then by
invitation, each week. And, broadly speaking, very friendly
people they transpired to be; human, fallible, only too ready to
acknowledge their shortcomings as parents. *("It should be me at
this school, not our Ken.")* Also they were very patient and
understanding, broadly speaking, with the 'new' ideas I
propounded to them: happiness more important than classroom
success; 'ethical' rather than 'doctrinal' assemblies; disavowal of
punishment; and sex education, according to his understanding,
for the youngest child. Why not?

To address The Problem of the Parent, I convened meetings at the
school. I cannot claim that I knew where I was going, only that I
must take a first step. I had some vague idea that I would give a
series of lectures on how to bring up children, in order to interrupt
the cycle of miseducation in parenthood. The discussion-mode,
however, took over from the earliest parent-Moot. The parents
listened attentively to me at first, and then to each other. They
asked me questions. They asked each other questions. They
swapped experiences. They contradicted and offered advice to
each other. They contradicted and offered advice to the 'lecturer'.

When I realised how little I knew about the subject of parenting, I approached the local college of adult education to enrol on a relevant course. There was none. There should be one, so, with the breath-taking chutzpa of youth, I offered to run a course on Education in Parenthood myself at the college. It was the first, I was told in 1972, in this country of the blind leading the blind.

The 'Problem' Teacher

Teachers in ordinary schools transferred children to our special school, and I became necessarily acquainted with them. They visited the school and saw that it operated on a quite different educational rationale than their own, but they did not seem to mind.

In due course, they were happy to enable the return of the erstwhile 'disordered' child to their schools. They cooperated in my research into the long-term effects of attendance at our unschool.

In the course of time, I convened meetings of my fellow-professionals to discuss themes such as The Early Identification of the Behaviourally Disordered Child, Co-attendance at Special and Ordinary Schools, and, of course, Education in Parenthood. Such was the interest generated that we needed to employ a larger room, then a larger hall, each time.

I thought, and feel now even more passionately, that our Education-in-the-head System is harmful to the human mind, yet I perceived in the individual teacher - and, especially, the headteachers whom I came to know best - a deep concern for the well-being of the individual child.

Taking Stock: the Day School

The odd thing was that Summerhill had been a byword for eccentricity and rebellion for forty years, and yet here our little school was, albeit non-attributedly, practising a fullblown summerhillery with hardly a word of dissent. Even Hansard contained an encomium for the unschool from one of our visitors, the Tory M.P.

So much for the practice; what about the before-and-after results? In the research referred to above, our colleagues in Ordinary School judged that Misbehavioural Indices were reduced by over 50%; and specifically delinquent factors by over 75%. (I had it on good authority that no other special school in the country was conducting such research at the time, so there is no means of knowing whether summerhillery is more, or less, effective than other methods of dealing with behavioural disorder.)

Taking Cover: From Day into Boarding School

I had thought of working till pensionable age with that Educational Authority, with my professional friends: the teachers, the social workers and the policemen. During the '70s, however, the caustic blight of behaviourism struck my specialism nationwide, and I was faced with the directive to abandon the Moot and adopt the 'token economy' of the Smartie.

I was a recusant to the prevailing orthodoxy, and relinquished my headship, of course.   I took to the priest's hole of residential schooling. Meg and I purchased the building which was to be our new unschool.   It would have been appropriate to mark my indebtedness to Neill by the naming of the school after him. But would it be politic? We decided to name it after the A.S.Neill of the nineteenth century, so Robert Owen House, or 'Rowen House', it became.   The building was so small that we had to forsake our co-educational principles, and it became a school for girls only.

Moot into Counselling

I will be candid: the Moot was the showpiece of the community, the stage-in-the-round of which I was the director.   No programmme, no script, and all of the actors did not invariably put in an appearance, but it could be mighty dramatic stuff as the damaged feelings of these pressured girls thundered and lightned away.

Then Meg, who had been sitting quietly for some years, made a signal change to the ethos of the community.   Before or during the morning Moot, her eye would roam around the circle, and pause on one or other child. Arising stilly, she would go now to clasp her hand and accompany her out of the Moot.   Both would come back after ten minutes, or half an hour, and sit down together hand in hand, the child quietly smiling.

Thus the emergent counsellor stole much of my thunder and lightning.   It was a less exciting Moot, but a much happier ommunity.   How did she do it? I never troubled to find out.   It was one area where I was not tempted to follow A.S.Neill into his 'P.L.'s, his 'Private Lessons'.   Each to his own.   I supposed that Meg's active listening were a kind of P.L., with Carl Rogers but without Freud.

Taking Stock Again: Residential School

For a couple of decades our several schools had been visited on a nearly daily basis by teachers, policemen, social workers and parents, and by a fair number of H.M.Is and educational psychologists.   (A sample of opinions of the latter profession were: "This place is magic"; "The warmest community I have visited"; "I can't tell the staff from the kids", and "Can't you make her go to class instead of lying curled up on the bed all day?")

Because of the advanced school-age of the young women referred, there was little chance of re-integrating them into the Ordinary school, so I could not research the before-and-after effects of their sojourns with us.

In 1962 I had written, "Had I only photographic evidence of [the changes in this child over several months] the rest of my essay were superfluous." So I took photographs of the children so often and so informally that they became quite accustomed to my camera-presence. The results tend to support my thesis.

Because of our rural isolation, I met the parents only occasionally, so I had to console myself for not being able to conduct seminars in Parenthood by establishing a play group within the premises to give our pupils, already young women on admission, practice in motherhood.

Due to the continued structured setting of the kindling-sticks, I had become accustomed over the decades to the child's spiralling from the 'disturbed' into the 'balanced' self. My epiphany in this community for young adults was the way in which the older child, the individual child-metamorphosed-into-adult began to take responsibility, at first falteringly then assuredly, for the newly admitted disturbed child. For instance, over a three year period, Rachel 'befriended' Nikki, Nikki 'befriended' Helen; Helen 'befriended' Liz; Liz inducted Paula, deeply phobic to school, into the community; and 16-year-old Paula became our first paid childcare worker.

As I witnessed such miracles I would take verbal snapshots in my notebook of events I observed or the words I heard. Later, I turned these episodes into written documentary 'stories' of startling unverisimilitude.

I gathered the anecdotes, including one remarkable series of spontaneous letters (written by a seismically disturbed child who is, in 1997, a senior childcare worker in a Local Authority children's home), and decided to publish them. What shall I call my press? It was due, after all, to the inspiration of Homer Lane and A.S.Neill - so The Laneill Press it shall be. At least Neill might have harrumffed his approval that because I am interested in education, none of the stories takes place in the classroom.

Doctrinaire or Pragmatic?

So, how relevant is Neill to me after a quarter of a century? Is my practice markedly different from his, given our different circumstances? I will be candid: I collect and cherish, but do not read, books by Neill. He is too repetitive, too prolix, too indulgent of his weakness for the boulversement de la bourgeoisie [the shocking of the middle-class mind-set]. The skilled editorial surgery of two Americans, Harold Hart (1960) and Albert Lamb (1992) has done him a service.

No, I prefer Neill the Man to Neill the Writer. The Man who speaks trenchantly, revealingly, as in the apothegms quoted on earlier pages:
'You won't want to visit the classrooms if you are interested in education' and

'Duncan is very polite, and he doesn't seem to be getting any better'.

Pure Wilde; pure Neill. But Neill was not, in fact, indulging in even Chestertonian paradox, much less Wildean wit. He was not trying to be clever. For once, he was not even trying to make a joke. He meant each word as it came out of his mouth, and as you may now read it on the page.

I am happy to agree to differ, not diametrically but tangentially, on minor principles, like smoking and swearing. I subscribe to Shared Responsibility rather than to Homer Lane's Self Government. The circumstances of my specialism made me, with great early heart-searching, more proactive with the bully, more ready to confront him, than Neill evidenced himself to be.
I did not feel the inclination to follow him into Reich, or even Freud, and no doubt I am the poorer for it.

If I did want to pick a difference with Neill's canon of beliefs, it would be with his declared attitude towards learning - another book-title, *Hearts not Heads in School*. When Neill affirms the right of every child not to be forced to learn, I stand shoulder to shoulder with him. These are days of massive marital breakdown, of endemic emotional illness, of prisons overfilling into the sea. So when Neill affirms the priority of emotional over intellectual learning - of the Heart over the Head - then I find myself hoarse at the barricades beside him.

But when he asserts, Hearts not Heads in School, then I must fall silent. Children have as equal a right to learn intellectually as emotionally. In an ideal world, I affirm the equal importance of Hearts and Heads in School.

So, to resume, if I had found that it had proved more effective to punish, if I had found that the homily were an effective method of instilling virtue, if I had found force-feeding more effective than the encouragement of academic appetite, I could not support Neill.   If, finally, I had thought that the exercise of my own authority would have proved more effective than my fostering of the authority within each child, then I should have renounced Neill with all his blinkeredness and his wrong-headedness.

In Johnathan Croall's excellently even-handed biography with its significant sub-title - The Permanent Rebel - we may read Neill's manifest human faults and errors of judgement. Notwithstanding, I declare that I would rather be wrong with Neill than right with anyone else.

Taking Stock Again: How Summerhillist?

As I have recounted, there were umpteen professional and lay visitors to Rowen House Unschool over a quarter of a century, to oversee and assay the care of scores of children. One of Her Majesty's Inspector of schools 'approved' it after six years. Another came and re-approved it two years later. This was very gratifying, and ensured our continued livelihood, but what did it mean? Had the educational establishment caught up with Neill that it bestowed such favours on one of his acolytes? (After all, in the wider educational field only a couple of decades after Neill's death, corporal punishment is abolished, the great majority of secondary schools does not have a religious assembly, and sex education is mandatory. Only the Berlin Wall of academocentrism and compulsory teaching remains standing... crumbling.)

The uneasy thought did occur to me from time to time: would Neill not have some misgivings about the official 'approval' of this man's practice? Was 'The Summerhill Idea', as distinct from 'summerhillery', inherent in his school at all? Visitors at about the same time provided evidence on two antithetical co-ordinates.

Two Visitors: The Historian and the H.MI.

The Historian

One visitor, John Shotton, the author of a history of libertarianism in education, did not spend much time talking to the headteacher. He seemed more interested in tape-recording conversations with individual children, and their child's-eye-views may be read in *No Master High or Low* (LibEd 1993). In one reference, he conjoined the two unschools as, *"the likes of Summerhill and Rowen House"*.
He continues:

> *"What unites [Homer Lane's] Little Commonwealth... and Rowen House... is the importance attached to personal*

> *autonomy, the aversion to systems of reward and punishment, hostility to coercive pedagogy and the fundamental and central belief in [shared responsibility]..."*

Thus, in a neat leap-frogging of the generations, the historian links the community which, in 1914, inspired Neill, with the community which, in 1979, Neill inspired.

Her Majesty's Inspector

The second visitor, the third HMI, new to the school and to the Inspectorate, did not record the results of any conversations she may have had with the children. At the end her day's visit, she addressed the headteachers, commending what she called 'the essential rightness' of the 'the warm and caring atmosphere' of relationships within the community.

She identified, however, 'grave shortcomings as a school', and required that:

- the National Curriculum be introduced;
- the Moot be expunged from the timetable; and
- attendance at class be strictly compulsory.

We did, of course, give it a try. We had, after all, a livelihood to earn, dependents to support. The researcher in me took a certain melancholy interest in viewing the effects of dismantling the glowing logs of the perceived 'essential rightness' of the 'warmth' of the community.

We removed the forum of the Moot. We 'encouraged' the pupils to attend class, but with an edge to our voices, and, in the end, brooked no refusal. We sawed and hammered out the fretwork of a revised timetable. We became less of an unschool, and, in good faith, strove to become a 'good school'. That we achieved a certain measure of success was reflected in the response of our several school phobics. They knew a good school when they saw one, and left.

Same staff. Different regime. Same children. Different atmosphere. So this is why teachers are taking early retirement in their droves from what must be one of the most richly satisfying of professions! So this is the fullness of my debt to Neill for my quarter-of-a-century career play-working in the vineyard of my specialism of bitter-sweet fruits!

One piece of before-and-after-the-Inspection evidence emerged. Sixteen-year-old Claire had written a letter to her M.P., and asked me for his address. Without tinkering with either its spelling or punctuation, I present this child's-eye-view of the improvements wrought upon our community:

12 February 1991

Dear Sir,

Regarding the relatively new school structures imposed by the DES following the introduction of the National Curriculum, I wish to voice my opinions upon the effect this has had in special needs schools and therapeutic communities.

The National Curriculum... has put a lot of undue pressure on the staff and girls. Most of the girls here have had problems at a "normal school", and come here to get away from that kind of atmosphere. The National Curriculum has meant that a number of members of staff who have much more important things to do i.e. counselling have had to spend a lot more time and effort on more trivial things like getting the girls to class and making them stay there, where as class used to be voluntary and you could decide whether or not you wanted to go, and you could work on your own, without girls of a lower standard slowing you down.

After being at Rowen House for over a year I have seen the change the National Curriculum has made on it. The staff have not had as much time to sit down and talk to the girls individually and people are playing up more in class, which hinders people who want to learn.

Every morning we used to have a moot which is a meeting where all the staff and girls are present. As a community we would sit down and discuss, usually in a civil manner what was going

*wrong and right around the school, i.e. a girl could moot another
girls behaviour towards her and something would be done about
it. Now... things are left undelt with and the girls don't get as
much say as to how they want things run.*

*So with the staff being more concerned with discipline than
therapy and counselling it seems like the whole school is being
dragged into being the kind of school most girls found it
impossible to cope with. I think the quality of life for us girls has
changed for the worse because of these rules.*

*Yours faithfully,
Claire*

It may be added that Claire had some experience of the 'good'
school, having attended twelve of them. She had misbehaved and
been "asked to leave" from several secondary schools, and spent
her last year with what she called 'The Thirteenth School ', before
entering university.

Sell out, or Sell up?

What were we to do? Sell out on the children? or sell up? We
sold up, of course. One man's practice of The Summerhill Idea
was over.

Epilogue: Summerhill Re-visited: 1996.

During the 1950s two young men had sprightly vagabonded about
the continent of Europe. They had become acquainted in a youth
hostel, and a growing friendship maintained beyond national
boundaries was bonded by a common love of languages. They
met occasionally in places as far apart as Seville, Geneva,
Alicante - and Leiston, in Suffolk.

One young man possessed little talent for languages (though his
love was abiding), and had to settle for the headships of schools
for educational disaffiliates.   The other was so skilled a linguist
that, as we have learnt, he became a Fellow of their Institute.
Among many other occupations, he worked at - and wrote letters

from - Summerhill for a season before he was invited to become principal of an alternative educational venture in the US of A.

In August 1996, after an interval of over thirty years, the two young men, both now greying and more settled of gait, converged again upon the Great Unschool for the 75th anniversary of its opening. One photographed the other in a series of embraces with his now middle-aged 'pupils'. They paid a visit also to that shrine of teacherly-love and child-initiative at neighbouring Burston, and called to meet its chronicler, Bertram Edwards.

During the intervening months there were the usual desultory telephone calls. Then, nine months in its gestation, a letter arrived out of the blue - the unplanned peroration to my essay.

May 14th 1997
Ay! Summerhill! What an effect that place has on people! I spent a mere 18 months there, and it has affected the rest of my life. Looking back over the years of a not uneventful life [as civil servant in Durham, vendangeur in France, butcher's boy in Geneva, wire-factory worker in Germany, telephonist in Seville, and headteacher in Vermont, the U.S.A., a restaurant proprietor in Barcelona, and a Europe-wide travel courier], if I were to pick out any period that was the most fulfilling in every respect, it would have to be the time I spent at Summerhill.

Going back to it last year was like a dream... Such pleasure just to be there again! Such emotion at meeting old friends who were young when I knew them! It was as though I'd never been away. And I suppose it was because Summerhill has never been far away from my thoughts over the years. I've lots of fond and vivid memories I'll never forget.

That's my way of saying 'Thanks Bryn'. If it hadn't been for you...

* * * * * *

Apologia

The writer who treats seriously of his subject usually assumes as a premise for his argument complete objectivity. I can make no such claim. I recognise that this essay, which started simply as the study of a school and developed, with growth of conviction, into a polemic about a way of life, has been influenced by unconscious and possibly illogical reasons.

I can only claim to have *aspired* to objectivity. Richard Jefferies again:

> *"Men's minds... are unlearning, the first step to learn. As yet we are in the fact stage; by and by we shall come to the alchemy, and get the honey for the inner mind and soul. I found therefore... [that] there were no books, and it came upon me, believe me, as a very great surprise... It is nothing but unlearning, I find now."*

He who would study Summerhill must 'unlearn' many of his assumptions before he can justly assess its worth. It is certain that within twelve months of writing this essay I shall have come to question the validity of many of the conclusions which I have arrived at in it, and ten years hence may disown them altogether; not so much because I shall consider them to be wrong in essence, but because I shall be able to set them against the broader perspective of wider knowledge and - more important - deeper understanding.

But 'conclusions' is, of course, the wrong word. I will no more allow it to be said that this essay contains my 'conclusions' about the subject than one can claim that a cupful of water scooped from a stream holds 'the current'.

Reading notes

The four books which have been the cornerstone of my understanding of 'the Summerhill Idea' are:

Summerhill, a Radical Approach to Child-Rearing, by A.S.Neill. Neill himself considers that he has written only four good books out of the seventeen published: *That Dreadful School* (1936), *Hearts not Heads in School* (1945), *The Problem Family* (1948), and *The Free Child* (1953). The book *Summerhill*, first published in the U.S.A. in 1960, and in England in 1962 is a compilation of the essence of these four books, and is the one to which I have referred most.

Education and the Significance of Life, by Krishnamurti (1955). This book navigates the higher reaches of educational philosophy, and is, in my opinion, a blueprint for Summerhill, although there is no reason to believe that Krishnamurti ever heard of the school.

Treatise on Parents and Children by Bernard Shaw (1910) A fine scarifying criticism of the state educational system, which, although dated in some aspects is still unfortunately not out of date. (It was sufficiently valued by one 'E.A.Blair' to donate a copy to his old school, Eton College, in 1920 (a fact not discovered until 1972, and disclosed by Orwell's biographer, Sheldon)

Tao Te Ching (The Book of the Way of Life) by Lao Tzu (c. 600 BC) Although this is not an 'educational' work, in the narrow sense we ascribe to the word, it is the book above all others which has helped me to understand the social implications of the Summerhill Idea; and, vice versa, the school Summerhill has helped me to a deeper appreciation of this Chinese classic.

Holmes Welch, in *The Parting of the Way,* his illuminating study of the Tao Te Ching, says:

> *"Lao Tzu wrote the earliest anarchist book in East or West. He has something to say to all who are troubled by the growth of the State. His book is also the earliest we have that explicitly recommends the policy of returning good for evil. Since it does so on logical rather than religious*

grounds, it has something to say to all those who would like to see that policy more widely accepted. Finally, here is the book, among all the world's scriptures, which addresses itself most specifically and radically to the problem of how to prevent war. Few people are likely to accept its proposals but many may want to know what they are."

And elsewhere:

"In Lao Tzu's opinion, [the child's] nature - his original nature - is free from hostility and aggression. But society mars this nature - and here Lao Tzu would seem to align himself with the extremists in progressive education. From the first parental whack to the last deathbed prayer, man is kneaded and pummelled, either by those who want to make him 'good' or those who want to use or destroy him. He becomes a reservoir of aggression on which society can draw to produce its goods competitively, fight its wars fiercely, and raise children more aggressive than himself."

I have quoted from Witter Bynner's translation of the Tao, except for one quotation which comes from that of W.G.Old.

A fifth strong influence during the writing was a fictional character whom I had first met during boyhood. He was factual - real - enough to my ten-year-old self, of course. If asked, I might have answered that the red-backed books were written by a chap called... yes, Richard Compton. Probably some relative of Denis. One puts childish things behind one, of course.

Years later, however, when I was finding my educational psychology course quite lifeless, I came across my boyhood friend once again.

Well, of course, I could see that the plots were sometimes creaking, and that some of the other characters cardboard, but William rose again magically alive and utterly real on the page. How could a Classics scholar, a spinster crippled by polio, have created such a boy? It came as no surprise to learn later that Richmal had helped to bring up her two nieces - and her nephew. This was a real boy. This was real child psychology.